Sunday River

 Sunday River

HONORING THE PAST, EMBRACING THE FUTURE

by David Irons

foreword by John Christie

Blue Tree
PORTSMOUTH

First published in the United States in 2009
by Blue Tree, LLC
P.O. Box 148
Portsmouth, NH 03802

37 10 1

Copyright © Blue Tree, LLC 2009.
Text copyright © 2009 by David Irons.
Foreword copyright © 2009 by John Christie.

All rights reserved. This book, or parts thereof, may not be reproduced in any form without permission from the publisher. The scanning, uploading, and distribution of this book via the Internet or via any other means without the permission of the publisher is illegal and punishable by law. Your support of the author's and photographer's rights are appreciated.

Printed in Hong Kong.

Library of Congress Cataloging-in-Publication Data available.
Library of Congress Control Number: 2009938614

Design: Brian Smestad
Text editor: Amanda Freeman

First edition, December 2009

ISBN-13: 978-0-9802245-3-5
ISBN-10: 0-9802245-3-5

For customer service, orders, and book projects:
Local: 603.436.0831
Toll-Free: 866.852.5357
E-mail: sales@TheBlueTree.com

www.TheBlueTree.com

Blue Tree
A BOUTIQUE PUBLISHING FIRM

There are many people to thank for this book, especially Dana Bullen, Sunday River general manager, and marketing vice president Jim Costello, who asked me to write it, but one person helped the most. For thirty years this person has put up with my pursuit of skiing and writing about my way of life. I have enjoyed her company on countless trips, and she has always been supportive when those trips didn't include her. She has been understanding when I put off items on the "Honey do" list to the time when the book was finished. Without her patience a lot of my work, including this book, would have been difficult. With her support I have had some success. For her loving companionship and being constantly by my side in so many ways, I dedicate this book to my wife, Pat. Thanks forever.

Foreword by John Christie	ix
Introduction	xiii
Chapter One: 1950s	17
Chapter Two: 1960s	31
Chapter Three: 1970s	41
Chapter Four: 1980s	67
Chapter Five: 1990s	87
Chapter Six: 2000s	101
Trail Map	112

Foreword

Sunday River has a storied past. It is fitting that the story now be told, especially by someone who has watched the story unfold from the inside of this remarkable resort.

My own memories go back to early meetings of the Maine Ski Council over forty years ago, and the powerful presence of Mike Thurston as a champion for the potential for ski area development in Maine in general and at his personal love, Sunday River.

His was the voice we heeded as we grappled with the issues that a brand-new industry was attempting to address, and his wisdom, foresight, and optimism both inspired us and informed virtually all our decisions.

We all watched the early cutting of the first trails, the carving out of an access road, and the construction of a base lodge as Sunday River, like all of Maine's emerging ski areas, attempted to overcome the problems associated with the absence of adequate financial resources, fickle weather, the reliance on volunteers to help out in the development, and the need to attract skiers in sufficient numbers to pay the bills.

The Sunday River of today rests on the shoulders of those early pioneers, and I am proud to have counted them as my friends.

But Sunday River as we now know it exists in great part as the result of the energy and vision of a single man, and the story of Les Otten's arrival, involvement, subsequent ownership, and ultimate development is one that nearly defies belief.

In the early 1970s, Otten came to Sunday River at about the same time I returned to Maine and bought Saddleback. We faced similar issues: survival owning a relatively small, local, partially developed ski area blessed with significant expansion potential on vast skiable terrain.

Sunday River as it appeared through the mid- to late sixties.

But Otten had three distinct advantages: the experience he had gained at Killington under Preston Smith that ingrained in him the importance of providing dependable skiing on well-covered, groomed, and appealing trails; the area's proximity to population centers that made it more accessible than his principal competitors in Maine; and, perhaps most important of all, a drive and ambition which, combined with his personal charisma,

provoked people to believe, and invest in, what he was attempting to do.

It would take a real insider to understand, and to tell us, the entire remarkable story.

Dave Irons is that authority, and we are blessed that he has authored the book that you are about to read, and that I found impossible to put down from the moment I read the first chapter.

But there are actually two Dave Irons who wrote this captivating story.

One is my old friend, fellow director of the Ski Museum of Maine, and the moving force behind, and a member of, the Maine Ski Hall of Fame. He's the Dave Irons who has long been recognized as one of this country's most prolific ski journalists since he broadcast his first report on radio nearly fifty years ago. In a broadcast and writing career that spans the intervening decades leading up to this book, he has authored over a thousand ski columns, articles, and stories that have appeared in newspapers and magazines read throughout the world.

The other Dave Irons is the lifelong skier whose history with Sunday River goes back to that first day the wheels turned on the original lift in 1959. Living in South Paris, he had cut his teeth on the slopes of Pleasant Mountain in Bridgton and welcomed the development of another nearby ski area, which gave him an option since, in his words, "Pleasant Mountain was getting too crowded." After a decade at Sunday River as a recreational skier, he joined the ski patrol and took over as director of the weekend patrol in 1971. He ran the patrol through the 1982 season and then skied with it on a limited basis through 1988. During the last four years of his ski patrol work, he served as an examiner for the Professional Ski Patrol Association. He continues to ski Sunday River from a house he and his wife, Pat, own in Viking Village.

It's rare indeed that an author of a book like this can be found who combines skills honed over a lifetime of writing experience with intimate, on-the-ground, firsthand, in-depth knowledge of the subject.

Fortunately, Dave Irons is such an author, and this is the book.

I invite you to savor the story and immerse yourself in the images as eagerly as I have.

You're in for a treat.

—John Christie

Introduction

When I was asked to write this book I readily accepted, thinking I knew nearly everything needed to compile the history of Sunday River Skiway. How wrong I was. Having been there on opening day, skiing the mountain as a recreational skier, and as ski patrol director, I had seen a lot firsthand, but as Paul Harvey told us there is the rest of the story. As I dug into that story I quickly realized that there were many people who played significant roles in the creation of the ski area and its growth over fifty years to a full destination resort.

Unfortunately, all but a few of the founders were gone by the time this project got underway in Dana Bullen's office Thanksgiving weekend in 2007. Fortunately, I was able to correct their dates. Jim Costello and Bullen thought the area opened in 1958, and I pointed out that the day was December 19, 1959. I could not have completed this project in six months, not while doing the rest of my work. I had to move quickly as Mike Thurston was in a veterans' home, Avery Angevine was 90, and Jack Trinward was in his eighties. Thurston and Trinward were part of the group that climbed the mountain in 1958. The rest were gone along with nearly all who built the ski area.

Starting down Ecstasy.

Fortunately, I was able to spend an afternoon with Avery Angevine and a few hours with Johnnie Rolfe's widow, Ruby, and son Red to get the full story on the construction of the original ski area. I found records at the Bethel Historical Society. Others were found with the help of Wende Gray in the attic over the offices at South Ridge, some of Ed Vachon's records were brought to me by his son Paul, and Walter Whittier's grandson Frank Whittier delivered correspondence that shed a lot more light on the transaction whereby Killington bought the area.

One thing I had reinforced was how many key players at Sunday River had gone on to important positions elsewhere in the ski industry. By phone and e-mail I contacted these people and received new insights into how things came together and challenges were met in the growth years. Bill Jensen is CEO of Intrawest, the multiresort company headquartered in Vancouver. Chip Seamans is general manager at Kirkwood in California where he lives with his wife Wendy. I contacted Burt Mills in Montana. Sepp Gmuender now splits his

time between Florida and his native Switzerland.

Several interviews, phone calls, and e-mails with Les Otten gave me more insight into the incredible growth years of Sunday River and furnished more names. I was able to follow up with Carl Spangler, now in Killington, Vermont, for the story of the train. Skip King filled in some blanks during his years, and Joe Aloisio provided valuable information on the construction years.

I was fortunate to have written the story of Maine Handicapped Skiing in a newspaper column when the program began. That made it easy to renew my contacts with Klaus and Beverly Salzmann, Meredith Elcombe, and Dr. Chip Crothers to update the story. I realized after it was written that I had left out Paula Berry Wheeler, who as executive director in the early years was an inexhaustible advocate and fund-raiser. Wheeler was surrounded by volunteers too numerous to name. There were also ski instructors who went beyond their normal duties to make the program work. Nat Putnam and Anne Friedlander were two who were especially dedicated.

I point these names out because I know that once this book is in print I will hear about others that I missed. That's inevitable over fifty years. Many people played a role at Sunday River, and not one was left out intentionally. As the publisher, Brian Smestad, told me, "That's what reprints are for." This being my first book, I have no idea how that process might work, but I would ask all who read this book, "If you have a piece of the story I have missed, please contact me and tell me your story." If nothing else, it can be included in later compilations of this history.

Finally, I would like to thank Dana Bullen and Jim Costello, who asked me to undertake this project to celebrate fifty years of skiing at Sunday River. For a year and a half I have been able to renew old acquaintances and in some cases make new ones. The memories, some in the book and a few that were better left out, were wonderful reminders of how much fun we had at Sunday River in the early years, with T-bars and a handful of runs, through the years of change and today's seemingly endless miles of skiing with great grooming and high-speed lifts. It has been a great learning experience, one that I expect will continue as readers of this book come forward. Enjoy the Sunday River story.

—David Irons

In the Beginning	19
The First Skier on Barker Mountain	19
Opening Day	23
Feeding the Skiers	25
Grooming, The Early Years	26
The Ski Patrol Gets Started	27

In the Beginning

Sunday River's first ski lift was actually erected on Vernon Street in Bethel, when as Mike Thurston puts it, "In the late forties about ten of us thought it would be nice to have a rope tow in town." Thurston volunteered to oversee it and having no idea where to start went over to Cannon Mountain in Franconia, New Hampshire, and made a few sketches. As Thurston later wrote, "None of us had any money to spare so we signed a note for $1000 with each ones liability limited to $150. We picked out a hill on Vernon Street and made arrangements with the owner to use it if we would repair the fence in the spring. It was all cleared with volunteer labor and Ad Saunders used his bulldozer to do a little rough grading. We also built a small warming hut. The daily and nightly fee was 50 cents so it was a break even operation, but, in fact, I think Howard Cole, the last volunteer president, had to pay a dollar or so to close the books."

That lift operated about ten years beginning in 1947, but unlike so many rope tow operations of that era it didn't simply go out of business. In the early fifties the group began to think bigger. While the Bethel area bustled with activity in the summer from visitors there to enjoy the rivers, lakes, and mountains, winters were quiet with only local citizens on hand and snowy empty streets. Something had to be done.

The First Skier on Barker Mountain

On a sunny February Sunday in 1958, a small group of men from the Bethel area gathered at a spot on Sunday River Road that is now the site of the Sunday River Inn. They included John Trinward, Addison Saunders, Murray Thurston, Howard Cole, Dick Walden, Stan Davis, Wilbur Myers, Vance Richardson, and Paul Kailey. On snowshoes they followed a logging road parallel to Barker Brook to what is now the location of the Barker Base Lodge. One of the group, Paul Kailey, chose skis with climbing skins. Their route up the mountain started up what is now Lower Cascades and wound up the mountain to the rocky ledge above the exodus of the Locke Mountain triple.

Once at the summit, steaks were cooked as the views of Mount Washington were enjoyed and discussions of the terrain's suitability for a ski area ensued. After exploring the summit, eight started back down on their snowshoes while Kailey removed the skins from his skis and became the first to ski what would become one of the early trails at Sunday River.

Mike and Connie Thurston, Sunday River's first family.

This excursion was a step in the process started in the mid-fifties by these men along with other local Bethel businessmen and members of the Bethel Chamber of Commerce. Their rate of progress was little short of amazing.

At a chamber meeting only weeks earlier, as the group was discussing the economy of Bethel in winter, the idea of a ski area was seen as a possible solution. Paul Kailey, then head ski coach at Gould Academy, suggested Barker Mountain as a possible site. He had observed the mountain as he had members of his student driving classes practicing in the area and as a longtime skier had thought of its possibilities as a ski mountain.

The *Bethel Citizen* February 13, 1958, edition reported that Howard W. Cole, local insurance executive, and state representative Addison C. Saunders of the Hanover Dowel Company were elected to the offices of president and vice president of the newly formed Bethel Area Development Corporation under the auspices of the chamber of commerce. Also elected were treasurer Edmund J. Vachon, president of the Bethel Savings Bank and assistant headmaster of Gould Academy, and secretary Guy Butler, owner and president of the Bethel Inn.

The board of directors included Kimball Ames, oil dealer, Philip Chadbourne, mill and land owner, Charles P. Chapin, local businessman, Richard L. Davis, mill and land owner, Stanley Davis, building contractor, Dana C. Douglas Jr., investor and surveyor, Henry Hastings, attorney, Charles Heywood, Murray Thurston, mill operator and chamber of commerce officer, John W. Trinward, dentist and chamber of commerce operator, and E. A. Van DenKerckhoven, telephone company owner.

This led to the formation in April of a committee consisting of Elwood F. Ireland, Gould Academy, Dr. John Trinward, and Howard Cole to select a committee to form a ski slope development corporation.

The Sunday River Skiway Corporation was incorporated on April 28, 1958, with a capitalization of 25,000 shares of common stock with a par value of $10 per share.

The foreword of the incorporation papers reads as follows:

> "The SUNDAY RIVER SKIWAY CORPORATION, hereinafter referred to as the Corporation was incorporated under the Law of the State of Maine, at Bethel, Maine, on April 28, 1958 to 'construct and operate for profit one or more recreational areas in the State of Maine, with major emphasis on winter sports, but not necessarily limited thereto.' Its present objective is the development of a major ski area, with all the necessary appurtenances, on Barker Mountain (sometimes called Bald Mountain) in the town of Newry, Maine, approximately five (5) miles from the business and shopping district of Bethel.
>
> Barker Mountain with an elevation of 2,582 feet and a vertical descent of approximately 1,400 feet, offers a variety of slopes that, in the opinion of several experts, will appeal to large numbers of expert, intermediate and novice skiers. With a good gravel road about a mile and a half length from the black topped Sunday River Road, an adequate parking area at the base of the mountain, a suitable lodge with all the necessary conveniences, a modern T-bar lift, and downhill trails that vary in length up to one-and-a-half-miles, the Corporation believes that Sunday River Skiway, when completed, will rank among the best in New England for scenic beauty, skiing pleasure and accessibility."

The papers listed sixteen residents of the Bethel area who had purchased 687 shares and would serve as directors. With the paperwork complete and a small treasury created by the

Looking across the valley.

John Rolfe.

original stock purchases, it was time to put the plan into action, and the board members of the new corporation moved forward on two fronts, raising money and planning the ski area.

According to Mike Thurston, the board figured that it would take $90,000 to actually get in business and they set up a plan whereby 90 percent of the money raised would go into escrow until the magic number was reached, leaving 10 percent for promotion.

When the fund-raising efforts stalled at $80,000 the prospects for the project going forward seemed dim, but Gould Academy stepped up to purchase $10,000 in stock, which met the $90,000 goal to move ahead with the project. As Mike Thurston put it, "They drove a hard bargain, asking for free skiing for all students, faculty and trustees in perpetuity." They settled for reduced rates for students, which Thurston indicated they would have probably given anyway.

As the stock sales effort progressed, so did developing the mountain. The mountain was owned by Penley Brothers Corporation, a clothespin manufacturer in West Paris, and a long-term lease with an option to buy was worked out so work could proceed.

The original idea was to lay out the ski area on the side of the mountain facing the future Sunday River Inn site, but before that got started they realized professional help was needed. Thurston knew Sel Hannah, a noted ski area designer, and inquired about securing his services. Hannah agreed to take on the project for the fee of $50 per day. That turned out to be a bargain, as Hannah drove from his home in Franconia, New Hampshire, to be at Thurston's home by 7:00 each morning and cruised the mountain until 5:00 p.m. He probably earned his entire fee the first day when he told the group that the face they were considering was too steep and moved the base to what is now the Barker Base area.

The trails he helped lay out are still among the most popular at the resort. They include Upper and Lower Cascades, Upper and Lower Sunday Punch, Rocking Chair, and Crossbow.

After determining where the lifts and trail should go, two individuals were brought on to do the actual work, both locals with the needed skills. John Rolfe, a logger, took on the task of cutting the trails, and Avery Angevine directed work on the base lodge and the parking lot.

To get power to the site during construction Angevine cut a deal with Stultz Electric in Portland for a 5,000-watt generator, once again a trade for shares. He and Howard Cole laid out the parking lot in less than two hours using a 100-foot tape and a carpenter's sight level. That original parking lot has seen almost no changes other than occasional grading in the off-season and each weekend is filled to overflowing by skiers who ski out of Barker Base.

On the mountain Rolfe and his son Eldred "Red" Rolfe were busy cutting Lower Cascades, a wide sweeping run that swung east from the top of the spot where the first T-bar would exit. A few hundred yards from the top a natural depression gave the run a brief flat spot before hitting a bump and traversing at a shallow pitch to a short headwall. Below that headwall the pitch lessened again before the final steep pitch back to the base. It was a trail that had everything, varying pitches, some double fall lines, and plenty of rolls. Once it opened, skiers discovered they could ski the run multiple times, choosing a different line each time. Years later those terrain changes made it an excellent race trail.

Next came Rocking Chair, a novice run accessed by unloading off the T-bar on a flat spot about halfway up the lift line, known locally as the "1,500 mark." This run allowed beginners to ride the T-bar and use the gently pitched trail that traversed to the west before broadening out for an easy run back to the base. Those two runs and a beginner slope by the rope tow would make up the entire trail layout the first year of operation.

To get equipment up to the cutting sites a Bombardier tracked vehicle was purchased. This was a far cry from the sophisticated grooming vehicles of today. As Red Rolfe put it, "They couldn't use it for trail grooming, they would have froze in it." But it served the purpose of hauling chain saws, gas, chains, wedges, and other tools up the mountain.

The idea was to get as much done as quickly and efficiently as possible. "We tried to cut the trees so they would fall into the woods and used a cable to haul the brush into the woods" was how Red expressed it. "We cut the stumps as low as possible and dynamited the rocks. Dad and I drilled the holes in the ledge and rocks and Roland Kneeland set the charges."

In the seventies, a generation of kids got to know Kneeland as the kind and caring gentleman who helped them onto the Mixing Bowl T-bar. None ever knew he was a specialist at handling explosives.

As trails were being cut, work was also progressing on a base lodge under the supervision of Avery Angevine. Working on a very limited budget, various building needs were met by trading for shares. Under this arrangement, Frank Lowell (owner of what is now Western Maine Supply) installed the foundation, Stan Davis laid the deck, and Hakken Olsen framed the building. Louis Sargent contracted to do the painting and coated the entire lodge and the lift shack in a single day. There was also plenty of volunteer labor. Jack Trinward, a board member and local dentist, spent a weekend pounding nails on the new base lodge and recalled, "It was a week before I could do any work in my practice, my hands were too sore." The end result was a 36-foot-by-60-foot, two-story lodge with restrooms and ski patrol located in the basement, which opened onto the top level of the multi-tiered parking lot. Office space occupied the end of the upper floor toward the pond by the Barker quad. Decks off the first and second floors faced the T-bar and Lower Cascades run out. A cafeteria and picnic tables filled the first floor with more picnic tables on the second floor. The original lodge is still part of the current Barker Base Lodge, although after many additions it's difficult to know exactly where that space was from the inside. Looking at the outside from the base of the quad, the low point of the vee in the roof marks the back wall of the original lodge.

To get skiers up to the base lodge, a road was needed, and it was decided to go up the opposite side of Barker Brook from the tote road used to reach the site in the beginning. That required a bridge over the brook, which Angevine designed and Rolfe built. Rolfe's son Red remembered, "We built the bridge with hemlock girders. We used log crib works with rocks behind them to support the bridge and channel the water. My father had built bridges for logging roads."

Later, Howard Cole told Angevine that the brook rising from heavy fall rains threatened to take out the bridge. Angevine directed a bulldozer to excavate a channel through the road to divert the water, and the bridge survived. It took a lot of work to replace the fill and restore the road, but it was a lot easier and less costly than replacing the bridge.

Two lifts were erected. The rope tow from Vernon Street was taken down and transported to the site where it was installed as a beginner lift along what is now the run out of Lower Sunday Punch. A 3,200-foot T-bar was installed up along the left side of what is now Monday

Mourning. At that time it was a narrow path up the mountain to an unloading station at the top of Lower Cascades.

Looking back, the scope of the project and the speed with which it went forward is admirable. From that winter hike in February 1958 to opening a ski area in December 1959, the Sunday River Skiway group had built a road, parking lot, and base lodge and cut trails and erected two lifts.

As the opening of the ski area approached in the fall of 1959, the project had exhausted most of the funds raised through the sale of stock. On October 22, 1959, the board closed on a $40,000 loan from the Small Business Administration (SBA), which guaranteed the operating expenses for the first season.

As with any loan application, a detailed description of the project was necessary and an inspection of the site was required. As part of this process, a representative of the SBA accompanied board members up to the base lodge area to see what had been accomplished and estimate the potential of the new ski area. One member, Charlie Bartlett, had the foresight to stash a bottle of Scotch in the brook to cool. As the story goes, the SBA loan officer received liberal doses of the chilled whisky and the loan was granted. A possible side effect of this technique is that it was many years before the SBA made another loan to a ski area.

Opening Day

December 19, 1959, marked the first day of operation for the Sunday River Skiway. There are no records of how many skied that first day, but we do know that snow had been limited that year and the only skiable terrain was the lower part of Lower Cascades and Rocking Chair. Skiers were instructed to unload at the 1,500-foot spot, a point halfway up the new 3,200-foot T-bar where the lift line leveled off a bit, making unloading easier. To the left they could ski the intermediate Cascades and to the right the novice Rocking Chair.

Riding the first lift in the sixties.

At the appointed hour a line of skiers waited at the T-bar ready to make the first runs. The first T-bar was occupied by Paul Kailey and his son Peter, with David and Peter Thurston on the next. The order after that is uncertain, but it is reasonable to assume that many skiers who had ridden the rope tow on Vernon Street were on hand along with other skiers from surrounding towns. I was part of that group, along with two skiing buddies, Jim Jackson and John Tucker, also from South Paris.

After fifty years no one could say how many runs they took on such limited terrain that day, but the memories of thin cover remain. Dave Thurston recalled the water bar at the bottom of the first pitch on Rocking Chair, which destroyed a number of the wood skis that were prevalent. Head's metal skis were available, but not many skiers had made the switch at

that time. Wood skis from Paris Manufacturing were more likely to be seen, with occasional Northlands or Kastles, although the sixties would quickly change that.

Another snowstorm or two allowed skiing from the top of the T-bar where there was only a single choice. Lower Cascades was much the same as it is today, a broad run making a long fall away left turn through a dip down to the top of a small headwall, referred to locally as the "Waterfall." Skiers could avoid this steep pitch by taking a short, narrow loop that passed the unloading point at the 1,500 mark before hitting a short flat stretch back to Cascades. They could also ski across the T-bar line to Rocking Chair, but skiing across the line was never recommended. Back on Cascades, the trail's pitch eased for a ways before the steep run back to the base lodge and the T-bar.

As Red Rolfe pointed out, the Bombardier used for transporting equipment while cutting trails in summer was not suitable for grooming as it had no heater, so the trails and T-bar line had to be foot packed that first winter.

In the base lodge every square foot was utilized. The cafeteria occupied the main floor along with picnic tables, with more seating and tables on the second floor along with a small office. In the basement a ski shop operated by Paul Kailey and his wife, Jean, a first aid room for ski patrol, and a garage were squeezed in along with restrooms. The following summer, the Kaileys built a small chalet on the opposite side of the Lower Cascades run out from the base lodge and the Sunri Ski Shop moved to the location it would occupy until the mid-nineties.

The Kailey's Sunri Ski Shop.

Jean Kailey sorting stock in the first ski shop.

Feeding the Skiers

One of the first needs was to feed the skiers, and the call went out to Barbara Godwin. In her words, "I had my own road side stand called Green Gables. Guess that's why they nabbed me for the first two years."

One of the most popular items was homemade brownies. Godwin remembered a woman whose name she thinks was Alice who made them the first year. Godwin got the job the second year but did have the original recipe, which is as follows:

Brownies

1⅜ cup Wesson Oil
6 squares of chocolate
2⅔ cups sugar
5 eggs
2 cups flour
1 teaspoon salt
2 teaspoons vanilla
1½ cup chopped nuts

Melt chocolate in the oil. Beat eggs and sugar together. Slowly add chocolate and oil to egg mixture. Beat well. Add flour and remaining ingredients. Bake in a 10½-by-15-inch pan at 325°F for 25 to 30 minutes.

Within a year or two of the ski area opening, the cafeteria opened and Dorothy York took over operation. Along with her sister Barbara Bryant, York saw to the feeding of Sunday River skiers into the seventies. In 1961, she bought Martha's Restaurant in Bethel, which opened for Mother's Day and closed in November when she switched to the mountain for the winter.

She described how the "donut man" would drop off three to ten dozen donuts each day, "Johnnie Rolfe would pick us up at 7:00 a.m. each day, we would load up the donuts and head for the mountain." Things were pretty simple: hotdogs, hamburgers, sandwiches, and french fries. "We tried to have something hot every day, hot soup or chowder."

Among her most vivid memories was the day she turned in the cramped kitchen area and somehow got her arm into the Fryolator. She credited an alert volunteer patrolman, Leo Lalemand, from Auburn, with preventing serious burn damage. He quickly led her outside and stuck her arm into a snowbank, cooling the hot fat and stopping the burning.

One of the biggest challenges was keeping enough trays available for hungry skiers to load up. Late in the afternoon each day, kids could be seen hiking up the steep pitch on Cascades in front of the lodge with cafeteria trays under their arms. Sliding down the pitch on a tiny tray was a real challenge, and more spills were seen than complete trips to the bottom.

The following summer, Johnnie and Red Rolfe were back at work cutting Lower Sunday Punch and Crossbow. Red recalled the challenge of working on the steep first pitch of Punch, felling trees so they would fall into the woods and using a cable to drag the brush into the trees. Today's skiers readily recognize Lower Punch as they cross it on the Barker Mountain Express quad, but many skiers have no idea where Crossbow is, a narrow run between Lower Punch and Monday Mourning. Crossbow, not much wider than the 210-centimeter skis of the day, was originally almost hidden behind the upper T-bar base building, but the addition of these runs gave skiers three choices off the top of the lower T-bar for the 1960–61 season.

Grooming, The Early Years

After a season of foot packing, the area bought a Tucker snowcat. Avery Angevine's brother Ernest built the first piece of grooming equipment in his shop, a giant roller to pack fresh snow. This eliminated the need for foot packers but did nothing when the packed snow turned to ice after a thaw. Angevine then designed and built a wood frame with spikes to break up the snow after it froze. Unlike the cats used today, the Tucker had no

A Tucker snowcat hauling one of Ernest Angevine's drags.

hydraulics and could only pull the various devices up and down the mountain. The U-blades seen on the new cats were a decade away and without hydraulics could not have been used on the snowcats of the day.

The Ski Patrol Gets Started

During the summer of 1959, the board of directors was busy arranging for everything from lift operators to cafeteria workers and recognized an important need. The new ski area would need a ski patrol. The only board member with a medical background was Jack Trinward, a local dentist, and he was assigned the task of recruiting and overseeing a patrol.

At that time the only requirement was a standard and advanced Red Cross first aid course, a total of twenty-six hours. Central Maine Power Company had many of its employees around the state trained as first aid instructors, and Erwin Lary of South Paris traveled to Bethel once a week to teach the course in a Gould Academy classroom.

This was Donald Angevine's introduction to first aid as a senior at Gould. Eight took that first course. Along with Donald were two Gould juniors, his brother Chris and Fred Lincoln, and Fred Desroches and Paul Bodwell. They patrolled weekends that first winter (1959–60) with no formal on-hill leader.

The following winter after deciding the University of Maine Orono wasn't for him, Donald Angevine was offered the job of full-time paid patrolman during the week and leader on weekends. After a couple of weeks of doubling as a lift attendant, he convinced management that he needed to be on the hill full time. As he described his position, "We looked out for safety everywhere, shoveling lift lines, checking trail conditions and taking care of an occasional injured skier."

The summer of 1961 saw the completion of a second T-bar, appropriately named T-2, which would haul skiers to the summit of Locke Mountain. This lift exited on the very peak of the mountain, a windswept ledge, with no protection from the wind and a clear view of Mount Washington. Skiers riding the Locke Mountain triple unloaded just west and below the spot where a lift shack (big enough for skiers to get in and warm up and chat with the lift attendant) was held in place by steel cables.

How bad was the wind? One day during my tenure as patrol director under Josef "Sepp" Gmuender, I called to request that we be allowed to close the lift as the wind was blowing the T-bars straight out. As we talked on the phone there was a loud "clang!" When Gmuender asked about the noise, I replied "A T-bar hit the tower." As we talked an even louder noise carried over the phone and again he asked, this time sounding a little anxious, "What was that?" I responded, "That one hit the lift shack." His quick response came, "Shut it down."

That same wind scoured the snow from the ledge and gave the patrol a constant challenge to shovel snow and cover the rock. When we had plenty of snow everything was fine, but in the early season the lift line had one large dip. When short or lightweight skiers traversed this section, they would find their skis lifted off the track, and often the result was a fall from the lift.

The view from the top of T-2.

Claus Wiese preparing to load chair.

Run out of Lower Punch.

This was an added challenge for the ski patrol as we used to return empty rescue toboggans to the top by slipping one side of the T-bar through a metal ring at the end of the handles and riding on the other side. That dip made this a real challenge, and on more than one occasion shorter patrollers had problems. After one lost sled, I issued an order that another patroller must occupy the T-bar behind the one carrying the sled. One day, Bob Harkins was riding alongside the toboggan and lost it. His friend and fellow patroller, Tom Walker, coming along behind, actually had to tackle the toboggan to keep it from cleaning out the skiers below. Fortunately, the dip eventually filled in with snow and no one was ever hurt by runaway sleds. With the insurance companies overlooking operations today, transporting rescue sleds in this fashion would surely not be allowed. In the sixties and into the seventies, running toboggans up lifts was part of our routine.

For Donald Angevine, the new lift created another concern. Skiing a couple of runs off the lower T-bar, it never took very long to reach an injured skier and move that skier to the aid room in the basement of the lodge. When he thought how long it might take to reach a skier on a two-and-a-half-mile run and how quickly hypothermia can set in, an extra emphasis was placed on communications to make sure the patrol was notified as quickly as possible to respond in a timely fashion. Many skiers are unaware of how a ski patrol works. In a typical operation patrol members are stationed at the top and are notified by skiers who relay the message through lift attendants. This is another reason to never ski alone. In the event of an injury someone needs to go for help. It may be a passing skier, but skiing alone on a trail not often skied could make that a long, cold wait.

Fortunately, that winter was also the year that Bob Walker joined the patrol along with Fran Renda. Renda was a veteran who had patrolled in Massachusetts and New Hampshire, and Walker, although new to patrolling, was a longtime skier and brought other skills. Walker had a workshop over the garage in his Poland home and was a skilled cabinetmaker who built finely crafted grandfather clocks. He used his expertise to build rescue toboggans, a number of which were actually still on the mountain into the seventies.

Some members of the ski patrol in front of their new building, 1972. Left to right: Craig Davis, Blaine Morse, Mark Daniels, Bart Bailey, Wyn Haskell, Steve Ayres, Doris and Dick Valentine, and Lee Irons. Kneeling: patrol director Dave Irons and assistant Leo Lalemande.

Through the sixties, the weekend patrol gradually grew in size with a local skier, Tom Yates, taking over as a full-timer working alone Monday through Friday and skiing with the volunteers on weekends. I joined the volunteers for the 1969–70 season after skiing with the patrol for the fabulous winter of 1968–69. Bob Walker had taken over the leadership of the volunteers.

Nils Torgeson doing the tip stand.

During the summer of 1970, Walker had an operation to fuse an ankle that had given him trouble for years from an earlier injury. He was still director of the patrol during the winter of 1970–71 but never skied that year and retired at the end of the season, which is when I took over as director of the volunteers.

While the first chairlift was being installed, the volunteer patrol was busy on another project. Sepp Gmuender told us that he would pour a concrete floor and buy the materials if we would build a first aid building. The building was completed just in time for the season opening and served the patrol until the building of the South Ridge Base Lodge. Naturally, the patrol needs to be stationed at the lowest point, which made a transfer to South Ridge automatic, and the patrol headquarters remains there to this day.

During those years, the director of the patrol was a volunteer who coordinated the annual refresher course and organized things on weekends and holidays. The ski area hired one individual to patrol the slopes during the week. With the low volume of skier visits, this system was adequate. A year after the purchase of Sunday River by Killington was completed and Les Otten was installed as area manager, the Killington system of incorporating ski patrol into "skiing services" was introduced at Sunday River. The name was changed to snow services and the idea was that ski school directors would also be in charge of ski patrol. The first under this system was Eric Paul, a PSIA certified instructor.

For the rest of the decade the weekend patrol operated as it had right along into the early eighties. When business started to grow and skier visits increased, more professionals were brought on board, a number coming from the Outward Bound program that had an operation in the Sunday River valley.

On to the Summit	33
Beginners Get a Break	33
Day to Day in the Sixties	34

On to the Summit

After two winters of skiing on the lower two-thirds of the mountain, a second T-bar was added, which would carry skiers to the summit. Because of the high winds scouring the bare ledge at the peak, the top shack was secured to the site with steel cables extended from anchor bolts over the top of the building. Those same winds kept the ski patrol busy shoveling snow back onto the ledge to protect the skis as skiers exited the lift.

Skiers riding the upper T-bar (T-2) were greeted with a spectacular view of Mount Washington, towering in the distance. That view inspired hundreds of picnickers over the years. A trio of new runs was now available. Upper Cascades followed the ridge to the east before dropping over a steep ledge at the bottom of which the run flattened out in a short cruise to join Lower Cascades. Looping around to the west, skiers followed Upper Sunday Punch, which would take them back to the base of T-2 or to Lower Sunday Punch. Another trail required a bit more effort as skiers continued west past the top of Sunday Punch on a flat, and in one place a bit uphill, as Lazy River traversed the top of the mountain before dropping in a narrow twisting loop back to the base.

The idea was to have an intermediate run from the top, but the narrow run with a few steep spots was quite a challenge for low intermediates. Lazy River did achieve one goal. Skiers choosing the two-and-a-half-mile trail were not back in a lift line as quickly as those choosing the more direct routes.

Having the two lifts also reduced lift lines as skiers quickly learned to decide their trails by the length of the lines. Skiers arriving at the top of the lower T-bar would eye the line on the upper lift. If it seemed longer than the one at the bottom, they headed back down Cascades. This also worked for skiers coming down the upper runs. A short line on the upper lift was a signal to ski just the runs off the top, while a long line sent them all the way to the base.

After that first year of skiing from the top it was decided skiers needed a way to access the new Lazy River run without climbing. A narrow path was cut traversing across the face of the mountain from the top of Sunday Punch to a spot on Lazy River. This shortcut, with its dips and rolls, was an immediate hit with the kids, but adults with longer skis and no room to turn found the run a bit challenging. It was aptly named Goat Path.

Beginners Get a Break

The rope tow beginner run had little use in the first years as newer skiers opted for the lower T-bar and the slightly more difficult Rocking Chair run. The ease of riding a T-bar instead of a rope tow more than offset any extra challenge of the ski run.

In 1963, it was decided to get rid of the little-used rope tow and give novices their own learning area. The Mixing Bowl T-bar started below the base lodge and ran to an unloading area near where the current South Ridge quad unloads. Skiers could swing left to the run out of Lower Lazy River or right to a new run, a broad gentle slope back to the base of the lift.

The new beginner area was an immediate hit. Not only was the pitch gentle and the T-bar easier to ride than those over on the mountain, but except for skiers occasionally taking a side trip after a run down Lazy River, the novices had the slopes to themselves. The segregation was a real benefit to both the instructors and the pupils. The run over to Mixing Bowl was an easy run downhill from the base lodge, and when the lessons were over, skiers could ski down Lower Lazy River back to the lodge.

One of the best features of the new area was a roomy shack at the top for the lift attendant. As with other jobs around the mountain, the right person was found to watch over the kids who flocked to the new beginner area. Willard Wight lived in Newry and each winter trained the chickadees and other winter birds to come to his shack for the seeds he put out. They would perch on the windowsills for the feast as the kids watched them while warming up. Wight also took the time to teach the kids how to hold still and let the birds come to them on warm, sunny days. A generation of Sunday River skiers grew up with memories of feeding the birds at the top of Mixing Bowl.

Day to Day in the Sixties

Once the Mixing Bowl lift was operating, the Tucker snowcat was at work grooming the trails, and the base lodge and cafeteria were feeding the skiers, the sixties was a period of small steps and keeping the fledgling ski area operating.

A ski school was established under Nils Torgesen, who filled the caricature of the Scandinavian ski instructor to perfection. He cut an imposing figure in front of the base lodge with his blond hair, tanned complexion, and pipe, and watching him glide down the mountain in the feet-together, swiveling style of the day attracted many to his lessons. Especially the ladies. A few of the more experienced skiers became instructors. As Connie Thurston expressed it, "We learned to teach under Nils's wing."

While the businessmen who founded the area dutifully headed for work at their varied businesses, many of their wives took their skis to the mountain for daily sessions with Torgesen or his other instructors. Some had skied a little, but as many took up skiing only as a result of the opening of Sunday River Skiway.

T-1 and base lodge on a typical weekend in the sixties.

Johnnie Rolfe, who had intended only to cut the trails and lift lines, had settled in as mountain manager. In truth, he was acting as general manager, although according to his wife, Rosalie, he never had that title. Once the Tucker snowcat was purchased, Rolfe became the first operator. "John worked all hours," said his wife, "I would sit in the car or ride with him because I didn't want him up on the mountain alone." It should be noted that in those days there were no radios in the cats, and with only a single grooming vehicle working, a problem meant walking down the mountain on a dark winter night. Kimball Ames worked at the local bank and counted the money. "John would take it home to recount it and make the night deposit," Rosie remembered.

Daily operation of the area involved families and the community. Among those staying on after helping build the area was Roland Kneeland. The man who set the dynamite to help clear ledge and rock from the slopes returned to assist the kids and novice skiers who flocked to Mixing Bowl as they loaded the T-bar. At the top, Willard Wight kept a hand on the switch as they off-loaded to make sure no one got caught as the T-bar was released. Wight was retired from the Maine Forest Service and as a true man of the outdoors, soon had the chickadees and other small birds that didn't migrate south for the winter coming around to his shack for lunch.

Over at the base of the mountain, Dottie York's father loaded the lower T-bar. Many of the local skiers recognized Leon Wilson, who had spent his final years as a game warden in the region before retiring. Hiking the nearby fields, woods, and mountains in search of the whitetail deer was how many of Sunday River's skiers got in shape each fall.

After Mixing Bowl, the next trail cut on the mountain was Cascades Cutoff. Originally cut as a way for skiers to bypass the steep pitch on Cascades, this soon became the area's featured bump run.

Next to be cut was Upper Cut, a run off the top that paralleled Upper Punch with a cut over to that run or a short direct option directly to the top of Lower Punch.

A brochure from the mid-sixties encouraged skiers with the following lures:

Approaching the top of T-2.

Short Waiting
T-bars in plentiful numbers mean surprisingly short waiting lines.

Professional Teaching
Uel Gardner, one of the East's most highly regarded teachers, instructs in the American Technique. And he knows how to customize his teaching to fit your ability. And this year the teaching area will be restricted, away from the main stream of traffic.

Ski Shop
Carries a complete line of clothing and equipment including the world-famous HEAD SKIS. Repairs and rentals also available.

Lodge
Pick your own relaxation. Lounge on the Sun Deck, or socialize with other skiers in the large, redecorated lodge.

New England's best novice area is the Mixing Bowl. A wide, wide, gentle slope that's not too long and not too short, with patient and courteous attendants to help you on the 2,600 foot T-bar. Learning to ski well is a pleasure in the Mixing Bowl . . . not too crowded yet you're never stranded by yourself.

The front of the brochure featured the blond Viking with his horned helmet on skis, the logo of Sunday River Skiway's early years.

This brochure also offered lodging specials and introduced the area's first foray into real estate. Viking Village was created along the west side of the access road just below the parking lot with lots on the access road, a loop road, and an inside road bisecting the center of the property. Viking Village was founded in 1965 and today has about forty homes, having become one of the most desirable locations at the now-expansive resort.

Avery Angevine recounted how he and Paul Kailey had argued whether the first lot in the village should go for $300 or $500. Walter Cherry became the first landowner in Viking Village for $300.

Over the next five to ten years a number of families purchased the lots and built ski homes in Viking Village, many becoming Sunday River season passholders. In no particular order, these included Mike Lynch (the only one who made Viking Village his full-time home after retirement and current manager for the village association), the Baileys, Whittiers, Wescotts, Knowles, Hodgons, Fullers, Delaneys, Stackhouses, Hannahs, Stevens, Kellys, and Cunninghams.

Other properties advertising lodging were The Barn (now the Riverview), Norseman Inn, Red Rooster Motel, Sudbury Inn, and Sunday River Inn. The Barn was converted from a milking barn by Mike Thurston and featured three-room family units sleeping seven, $20 per night for four.

One regular at The Barn was Bim Simmonds, who had a trail named for him (Bim's Whim between the top of Locke and White Cap) and a conference room in the Summit Hotel.

The Norseman, owned and operated by Claus and Jacki Wiese, offered Scandinavian hospitality modified American plan (MAP) from $9 and imported Norwegian gifts.

The Red Rooster Motel had MAP $8, European plan (EP) $8 single to $14 double, hosted by Phillys and Rollie Glines. The Sudbury, operated by June and Norm Greig, had MAP $7.50 to $9.50, and the Sunday River Inn offered MAP from $6.

That brochure didn't mention prices, but we do know that by the end of the sixties the daily rate had not passed the $6 mark. That meant weekend skiers from away could stay and ski in Bethel or Newry for as little as $12 with breakfast and dinner included.

In 1965, Fred Burke received his discharge from the U.S. Army where he had served in Germany in Special Forces, a connection that would help the area a few years later. By then Uel Gardner had branched out and was directing ski schools at the now-defunct Poland Spring area, Mount Abram, and The Balsams in addition to Sunday River. During the winter of 1965–66, the former Green Beret worked as an instructor under Gardner, working summers to develop his new Sunday River Tree Service. When the board of directors expressed the desire to have a ski school director devoted only to Sunday River, Gardner left to focus on the ski school at the new Balsams Wilderness ski area and Fred Burk took over the ski school for the 1966–67 and 1967–68 seasons. Unfortunately, a decision by the Maine labor department that would have combined his instructors and tree workers under workmen's compensation and unemployment made it impossible to continue profitably.

For the 1968–69 season, the board hired Butler S. "Larry" Cox as general manager and Gary Keidaisch was brought on to direct the ski school. That was a fortuitous year for both Cox and

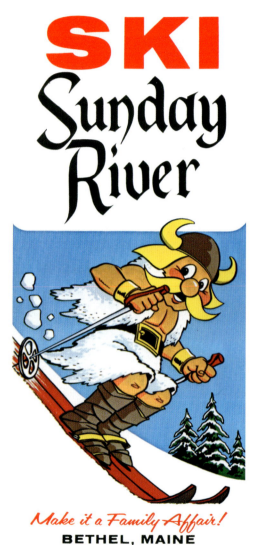

The first brochure introducing the Viking.

Keidaisch. While most of the sixties had been a struggle, that changed in 1968 when the snow came early and often.

By Thanksgiving of that year, close to three feet of snow had fallen and all ten trails and three T-bars were open in early December. The snow continued through the winter with sixty-six inches in February and no thaw of any kind all winter. Exact records are not available, but Mount Washington had five hundred inches of snow that winter and Sunday River had to be close to three hundred. The loading area of the upper T-bar had to be shoveled out, and by mid-February skiers loaded the T-bar next to a snowbank that was over their heads. By spring, cars had bumper stickers proclaiming, "We survived the winter of 69."

Gary Keidaisch turned out to be one of the most accomplished skiers to head the ski school. He was named to the eastern PSIA demonstration team and was presented an offer by Hart Ski Company that he couldn't refuse. This led to his performing on ski decks at ski shows and ultimately to a very successful career as a ski rep. Following his success in equipment, he turned to the resort side and became president of Stowe, one of the first in a sizable list of talented individuals who would work at Sunday River and go on to important jobs in the industry.

The 1968–69 season was the most profitable year for the young ski area, and dreams of a chairlift sprouted. There were numerous ski areas with T-bars, but to be considered a major area, aerial lifts were required. Cannon had a tram since the late 1930s. Pleasant Mountain and Mount Abram had chairs, and Sugarloaf and Wildcat had gondolas. Sunday River needed a chairlift, and that summer and fall a lift line was cut for the first chairlift. But the funding was not available, and the 1969–70 season was another of riding T-bars. Jim Hinman was brought on to replace Keidaisch as head of the ski school.

The snow didn't come as early that year, but a major storm hit just before Christmas, allowing the area to open with a foot-and-a-half of fresh snow. Skiers went to bed Christmas Eve thinking a repeat of 1968–69 was beginning. Their hopes were washed away when the snow turned to rain and the deluge soaked into the snow. A hard freeze followed, and the mountain turned to ice. In those days before snowmaking and power tillers, the only relief would come from more snow, and it was scarce that winter.

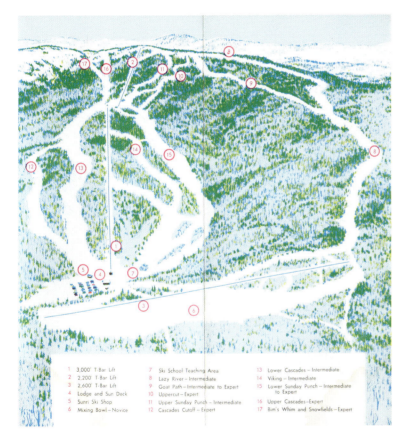

Trail map from 1965 to 1971.

The best day of the season came late. While the skiers grabbed what skiing they could find on the regular trails, what snow fell had been left to accumulate on the new lift line. Through freezes and thaws that snow had set up, providing firm base. When the sun softened the surface, the run was opened for the first time in late March, and the skiers attacked it. One reason it had not been skied was that before the chair it wasn't that easy to get to. Other than the route

to Lazy River, either across the top of the mountain or Goat Path, skiers would not even see the run from the top. They had looked up from the spot where it entered Lower Sunday Punch and certainly wondered about skiing it. That was before the trail was named Agony, and that day with soft spring surfaces and no moguls it was anything but.

One tradition created in the sixties was the mountaintop picnic and barbecue in the spring. In late March, Sunday River regulars would gather on the ledges at the top of the upper T-bar to celebrate the warm sun and spring skiing. It would become easier once a chairlift was installed, but somehow these skiers managed to get grills, charcoal, food, beer, and wine to the summit via the T-bar. Some of these things no doubt road up on rescue toboggans manned by willing ski patrol members.

One of the most enthusiastic couples at these spring gatherings was Claus Wiese, a board member and president of the corporation in the early seventies, and his wife, Jacki. To Wiese, skiing was always a celebration, and he was easily recognizable in sweaters from his native Norway. Some were happy with sandwiches, but an equal number were grilling. In addition to the usual hamburgers and hot dogs, there were sausages and even steaks. They would start gathering in late morning, and for some the party would last through the afternoon. Most were judicious in their consumption of adult beverages, but occasionally the ski patrol would be called on to give someone a ride down at the end of the day.

Fred Burk and his ski school.

On one occasion a group of Gould students had their own party away from the adults and some managed to overconsume. One young woman, who shall remain nameless, had reached a state where she could hardly walk and certainly was in no condition to ski down. When the lifts closed and the patrol gathered at the top for sweep, she was tied into a toboggan and Wyn Haskell, who truly enjoyed seeing what speeds could be reached, was given the handles. We saw plenty of air under the sled as it flew over the waterfall on Lower Cascades. When Haskell brought the sled to a halt in front of the base lodge, the young lady was helped up out of the sled, pale but sobered. Interestingly, she later married one of the ski patrolmen. I'm sure she remembers the ride even if the details of getting in the toboggan are a bit hazy.

As the sixties came to an end, Sunday River Skiway had completed its first decade with a lot accomplished. The trail mix was attracting a lot of skiers, and the area had a solid following, but to grow more was needed.

The Seventies and Big Decisions	43
Traditions, Born and Ended	46
The Biggest Decision	47
Burt Mills Arrives	49
Green Berets Find a Skiing Home	55
The Boston House, Party Central	57
Can Ams and Streaker	58
The Three Eras of Les Otten	63

The Seventies and Big Decisions

The first decision of the seventies was to bring on Josef "Sepp" Gmuender as general manager in the summer of 1970. Claus Wiese had been elected president by the board and was the one to direct things as the new general manager got started. The Swiss native wasted no time in moving forward. He had experience operating ski areas, coming to Sunday River from Glenn Ellen (now Sugarbush North) in Vermont, and he had definite ideas on how to succeed.

In September he presented a report that outlined the need for snowmaking and how to get it done. He stated the purpose: "The ski business has advanced to the top in winter recreation. More and more ski areas are mushrooming out of the mountains, and the competition is getting more significant as the years go by. A ski operation has to be able to compete with the growth of the ski business and cannot afford to stay back. This, naturally, costs dollars which have to be produced out of the operation. Considering the above, every ski area has its own way of drawing skiers, a ski area knows that a long season is the ultimate goal for success."

He went on to point out that in normal years the area would have frost and low temperatures for snowmaking by mid-November, "We can guarantee skiing for all of December, and especially for Christmas and New Years season, which is the most important time for us to produce a very substantial income." Gmuender further noted that figures from past years indicated Sunday River needed December operation to pass from red to black in the years to come.

His proposal was to install snowmaking on Mixing Bowl to make Sunday River the only ski area "this far north in Maine with snowmaking." He explained the art of snowmaking and the procedures involved and laid out a budget for installation and operation.

The material list included a water pump, hose, pipe and fittings, a diesel engine, a pump house, and other items totaling $20,063.40. Installation and manufacture of the snow guns added $2,240 for labor, machinery, and earth-moving equipment, running the total to $22,303.40.

His estimate for operation included seven days of continuous twenty-four-hour operation, which he felt would be sufficient to provide a good base on the proposed slopes. The total for compressor rental, fuel, and labor came to $4,313. The operator at $2 an hour would work 168 hours for $336, and his assistant at $1.80 would get $302.40.

Gmuender proposed that the payback in a year with no natural snow before December 24, including an increase in season passes, would be $14,000 by December 20, and another $20,000

Sepp Gmuender and Governor Ken Curtis look on as the corporation president, Claus Wiese, speaks at the dedication of Sunday River's first chairlift.

for Christmas week. Gmuender also brought in Erna Bezick to direct the ski school and Patrique Whale as race coach.

The snow guns were fired up as soon as temperatures dropped to sufficient levels, and the goal of a Thanksgiving opening was met. Over seven hundred skiers showed up to ski opening morning, and Gmuender had to call local radio stations in the late morning to announce that no more tickets could be sold. That total exceeded his projections through December 5, and the 1970–71 season was off to a great start.

Another benefit of the guaranteed skiing was being able to attract the 10th Special Forces training program. In his manager's report following the 1970–71 season, Gmuender cited the presence of the Green Berets as not only keeping the employees busy through January and February, but also helping to carry operating expenses for the period.

Trail and lift layout through the 1970s.

The season-end statements for the years 1969, 1970, and 1971 demonstrated the ups and downs of the ski business and the dramatic success of the snowmaking. Day ticket sales for the season ending in May 1969 were $92,162. They dropped to $37,045 the next year with poor snow, but rebounded to $80,610 following an early opening with snowmaking and good snow the rest of the 1970–71 season. Still, the profitability needed to impress the banks was not there and at the time of the season-ending report President Wiese stated, "The road proposed to follow by Mr. Gmuender, with the board's backing, is a challenging one and not without hazards, yet there is very little to do. We must break away from the vicious cycle of rising cost and diminishing return. I wish I could at the time of this writing state for certain that the arrangement for a chair is firm. New avenues for financing are tried every day, and will be continued until reached. Hopefully, we can report to you at the annual meeting that a solution has been found. If not, there is another year, even though time is running rather short. The sooner Sunday River can fight itself out of this financial maelstrom the better."

Gmuender was moving ahead, as indicated by this paragraph in his year-end report to the board. "To be in competition with all the ski areas around us and in competition with the ever-growing expenses, Sunday River must, as soon as possible, install a chairlift and develop long novice trails. The skiing trend has changed from an expert skier to a family-type skier. We at Sunday River have very limited trails and slopes for this potential skier and income."

Even considering how quickly he had been able to get his plan for snowmaking approved and carried out, the challenges of his new plan were daunting. Cutting the long novice trail was started out with a run that would circle beyond the Lazy River. The run was simply named for its length, the Three Mile Trail. The ski patrol that had to sweep the almost-flat run had another name for it, "the Big Mother."

The chairlift was another matter, but Gmuender was up to the task. He went to a company new to the business of building ski lifts, Pullman Berry. Those old enough to remember the days of extensive train travel remember the famed Pullman railroad cars. It was the biggest name in railroad passenger travel.

Gmuender related how he had spent two weeks doing the profile of the terrain for the lift design and taken it to Switzerland, where it became the first lift profile "pushed out on a computer." But the biggest factor in his words was "We got that lift from Pullman Berry for no money down."

Gmuender remembered the challenges of getting the lift installed in a short period of time, "We had to blast rock out to make room for the upper lift terminal, then we brought in a helicopter to set the towers."

The meeting of loggers hauling wood off Three Mile Trail and the helicopter pilots provided some interesting moments. On one occasion, a fully loaded truck was about to pass by the chopper sitting on the causeway between the base lodge and the pond. The truck driver was apparently unconcerned that the top of his load might clip the sagging rotor blade, but the pilot got his attention by asking, "Do you know that blade cost $5,000?" That was probably half the value of his truck, so he waited while someone climbed to the top of his load and held the blade up while he eased under it.

The deadlines were met, and in October then governor Kenneth Curtis joined Gmuender, Mike Thurston, and Claus Wiese on the upper deck of the base lodge for dedication. A small crowd of skiers and season passholders had gathered for the event.

That season's brochure was headlined:

Another tower goes up.

> A new look
>
> A new day is dawning at Sunday River.
>
> We've recently installed a new 5,100-foot double chairlift. It carries you quickly and comfortably to the top of the mountain where you'll find enough well groomed trails to satisfy every type of skier.
>
> Our new novice trail runs from the top of the mountain with a descent so gradual that even a beginner can experience the real thrill of skiing. The new trail averages 80 feet wide to provide plenty of maneuvering room.
>
> There are other exciting plans on the drawing board for the future. Under the direction of Josef "Sepp" Gmuender, general manager, Sunday River is continuing to grow and develop in order to provide the best skiing ever.

The brochure also contained a trail map showing the new chair and the new novice run. An all-day adult weekend lift ticket was $7, half-day $5, and midweek $6 and $4. A T-bar-only ticket cost $6 and a Mixing Bowl-only was $4.50. A special offered skiing Monday through Friday, including a one-hour lesson each day, and it was good at either Sunday River or Mount Abram.

The new lift changed the way skiers moved around the mountain. With the top terminal located west of the top of T-2, skiers would now access Lazy River without climbing, making that run a lot more popular. They could also vary the run by taking the first part of Three Mile Trail and dropping down a short chute to Lazy River. Another option was to take the new long novice trail all the way. Three Mile Trail circled around behind North Peak, reentering Lazy River just above Mixing Bowl with another lower branch directly to the beginner area.

A relatively flat run with just enough pitch to get there (now called Jungle Road), allowed skiers to reach Upper Cut and Sunday Punch from the chair. And, of course, the run under the new lift was now accessible, although left ungroomed. That year it was simply the lift line. The narrow run with a double fall line in places made grooming difficult at best.

Traditions, Born and Ended

Sepp Gmuender understood that skiers are a fun-loving group and enjoy exhibitions, parties, and celebrations. One such exhibition took place each Saturday afternoon when the ski patrol finished sweeping the trails. As skiers turned to get up to the T-bar in front of the base lodge, a ridge was built up, making a nice kicker by the end of the day.

Once the slopes were clear, it was safe (at least for other skiers) to schuss the last pitch on Lower Cascades and jump off that kicker. It was a horrible place to jump, as the landing was on a sidehill. Worse, jump too far and the landing would be flat. But the crowd gathered on the deck loved it as Gmuender would sit in his office and actually announce the event on the public address system. A bunch of kids would gather at the top of that final pitch, and joining them would be patrol members and an instructor or two not needed to sweep other turns. One by one they would fly down and hit the jump to the cheers of the après ski crowd. There were some great crashes, including one in late spring when a patrolman went too far, skied off the snow, and did a face plant in mud. It was called Lift House Leap, but the tradition came to an abrupt end when Tommy Walker got an especially high jump and had to duck to miss the communications cable that went from the base lodge to the lift house. It took his hat off, and Mike Thurston, president at the time, came off the deck and said, "That's it. No more." It was the end of a tradition. No one ever got hurt, but it really was an accident waiting to happen.

Another tradition is still celebrated each spring, "Pond Skimming." Sepp Gmuender started this his first spring. A hollow was bulldozed in the snow between the base lodge and the pond and filled with water. Skiers started up on Rocking Chair and tried to ski across the pond without sinking. A small jump before the pond allowed skiers to land in the middle as they tried to soak the crowd. Some wanted to make a big splash while others wanted to stay dry. A few patrolmen got involved. Bob Harkins (who would later create Perfect Turn) convinced his girlfriend to ride a toboggan, which he thought he could glide across the pond. Unfortunately, he had to let go of the handles halfway across in order to make it, and she was left in the middle of the pond on a sinking sled.

But that was nothing compared to the performance of Bart Bailey. Bailey, who loved speed and air time, figured if he started high enough up he could clear the pond. He almost made it, skipping off the water just short of the other side. That wasn't good enough. He went back up and started even higher. This time he cleared the pond but not the far bank. His skis plunged into the snow, and he cartwheeled into the ski racks near the base lodge. Claus Wiese caught the whole crash on film. Bailey wasn't hurt but did win the Sunday River Ski Patrol Crash of the Year Award.

The Biggest Decision

Following that 1971–72 season, Sepp Gmuender left, first to install lifts for a lift company and then to take over as general manager of Ski Roundtop in Pennsylvania. By then the founding directors were thinking their job was done, and they considered getting out of the ski business by putting the area up for sale. A new general manager was hired. Ray Starr's biggest job would be to arrange the sale of Sunday River.

Gmuender retained his interest in Sunday River and brought the area to the attention of his new employers at Ski Roundtop. Through the summer and fall, a series of letters from Walter Whittier, CEO of Hannaford, a stockholder, and avid Sunday River skier, were with officers of Ski Roundtop and Sherburne Corporation, parent company of Killington. Both companies visited the area, and both made offers. In the end, a special meeting of the stockholders was called for October 12, 1972, in Bingham Hall at Gould Academy. The purpose was to authorize the directors to sell 13,000 shares to Sherburne Corporation for $7.45 per share. Ski Roundtop's bid was $5 per share.

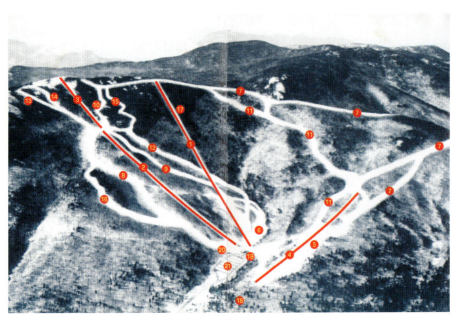

The first trail map with a chairlift.

LIFTS
1. 5,100' Double Chairlift
2. 3,000' T-Bar Lift
3. 2,200' T-Bar Lift
4. 2,600' T-Bar Lift

TRAILS
5. Mixing Bowl — Beginners, Novices
6. Ski School Teaching Area
7. 3 1/2 mile Novice Trail
8. Lower Cascades — Intermediate
9. Crossbow — Intermediate
10. Upper Sunday Punch — Intermediate
11. Lazy River — 2 1/2 mile Intermediate Trail
12. Lower Sunday Punch — Intermediate to Expert
13. Bim's Whim — Expert
14. Upper Cascade — Expert
15. Upper Cut — Expert
16. Cascades Cutoff — Expert
17. Chairlift Line — Expert
18. Cross Country Ski Trails

FACILITIES
19. Lodge, Cafeteria
20. Sunri Ski Shop
21. Parking Area

That fall of 1972, the Sherburne Corporation, owner and operator of Killington, Vermont's largest ski area, purchased a controlling interest in the mountain. A twenty-three-year-old graduate of Killington's management training program was sent over as assistant manager. Leslie Otten spent the winter of 1972–73 learning about Sunday River and its operation under Ray Starr and developing plans for needed improvements. Following that season, Les Otten became general manager at age twenty-four.

The first project was a big addition to the base lodge that doubled the interior floor space. The cafeteria was completely rebuilt with new equipment installed. Offices were moved to the basement from the cramped space on the third floor.

Eric Paul, a Bethel native who had grown up skiing Sunday River, was hired by Ray Starr to direct the ski school and showed up at the mountain not knowing about the change of managers. Paul, who had been teaching skiing at Pleasant Mountain (now Shawnee Peak), recalled walking in and asking Otten, "Who are you?" Otten introduced himself and asked the

same question, to which Paul replied, "I'm your ski school director."

Eric Paul then became the head of snow services, a new concept brought from Killington that combined on-hill services, including ski school and ski patrol. It would be the next season when that actually became functional.

Apprehension for the early season was featured in an article on December 3, 1973, in the *Portland Press Herald* headlined, "Open gas stations are scarce." Then president Nixon had requested gas stations to close on Sundays, causing skiers to wonder if they would be able to buy gas for the ride home after a weekend of skiing. This was the first gas scare of the seventies, but it didn't have as much effect as another matter.

The winter of 1973–74 was known for its lack of snow, with a number of areas opening only on a limited basis and nearby Mount Abram unable to operate for a good part of the winter. Sunday River, just ten miles up Route 26, was open continuously, if only on Mixing Bowl much of the time. That run was covered with man-made snow and open by Thanksgiving and stayed open every day, except for a few weekdays when no skiers showed up to buy tickets. There were times when the upper mountain opened, and finally in late March, natural snow provided skiing on the main mountain for the remainder of the season.

The fact that even good skiers showed up to ski with only the beginner area open made the case for more snowmaking, and the result was Killington's biggest contribution in the seventies. During the summer of 1974, a new trail was cut called Ecstasy and the chairlift line was renamed Agony, playing on a popular movie that year, *The Agony and the Ecstasy*. The new run ran diagonally across the upper mountain from the top of the chair to an intersection near the bottom of Upper Sunday Punch and on down to Lower Cascades. This made it possible to run snowmaking pipe in one continuous arc from the base to the top of the chair and open a one-and-a-half-mile run with 1,500 feet of vertical drop whether it snowed or not.

An ad ran in the *Boston Herald* on November 6, 1974:

> 1,500 vertical top-to-bottom snowmaking
> Maine's longest ski season last year, 159 days
> Full short ski (GLM) instruction program
> 1/3 down. 1/3 a month season pass payment plan
> 180 miles from Boston

The tag line read, "The best kept ski secret in New England."

Burt Mills Arrives

During Les Otten's first year as general manager, a new employee arrived who would later play a key role through the struggles of the seventies, the growth of the eighties, and into the expansion years. As Burt Mills tells the story, "I showed up during the winter of 73–74, got a part-time ticket checking job and got asked to help Odd Lyngholm to repair a broken Pisten

Bully 140 at the base of T-2. Odd had a way of using a sledge hammer for many fine mechanical jobs. I told him with some pretty frank language that if he used the sledge on a particular shaft that I was heading down the hill. He said 'Fix it yourself then, I have to fix the clutch on the T-2 motor.' I fixed the spindle and drove the vehicle to the lift base where I found Odd hammering on the clutch. He told me to drive the machine to the shop. I did this and figured that my employment was over. I didn't figure you could tell your newly acquired boss what to do and where to do it and still have a job. I went home and two days later got a call asking, 'Where have you been?' The ski company was evidently pretty desperate for staff. Also, as time went by, I grew a greater appreciation for Odd's sledge hammer. There was no end of crises to conquer and things to beat apart and beat back together again just to get by for another week."

Mills was quickly introduced to every aspect of operating a ski area. "My next tasks were to learn grooming and vehicle maintenance. I was tutored by Jim Sysko, whose idea of teaching was, 'follow me.' I recall many times seeing his taillights disappear in the distance and wondering what the hell I was doing there. I had no idea what it was like to ski, how to drive the machine, how to groom snow, or where the trails went! We dragged Otto Wallingford's (the owner of Lost Valley whose invention of the Powdermaker revolutionized grooming) Powdermakers behind the grooming cats, and with the race track mentality that I developed chasing Jim around, they were taking a beating. Frequently, I would find myself in a place where I was in way over my head from an ability standpoint, and I took many long uncontrolled slides off headwalls and occasionally into the woods. Needless to say, some of these deeds required rescue, repair, and plenty of swearing. I was given the opportunity to stay during the day to patch and weld the equipment. I had never welded in my life, didn't know where to start and wasn't very successful. The first few repairs I made might have lasted the next shift, or maybe if lucky the week."

I was directing the weekend ski patrol during the seventies and on one of those occasions, an attempt to groom Agony with its double fall line resulted in a grooming machine sliding sideways off the trail. The machine came to rest with a fir tree between the Powdermaker and the Pisten Bully immobilizing the groomer. Tommy Walker, a patrolman, was given the task of skiing down to the machine carrying a chainsaw so the tree could be removed and the vehicle freed. That incident was one reason Agony was left as an ungroomed bump run.

That summer of 1974, Mills learned about cutting trails and installing snowmaking when he was part of a crew that built the first snowmaking on Barker Mountain. "We cut Ecstasy and

Loading the chair in the seventies.

laid pipe from the top of the Barker double down the new trail and Lower Cascades."

In November 1974, an article in the *Maine Sunday Telegram* told how snowmaking to the top of the chairlift and a new trail to the top of the lower T-bar were the big additions for the new season. Les Otten was quoted, "We can now open Mixing Bowl in twenty-four hours from bare ground." It went on to point out that the dual system was designed to run both on the main mountain and Mixing Bowl simultaneously. With no natural snow, the area could have skiing on the beginner's area and a one-and-a-half-mile run from the top of the mountain.

Creating another trail.

The base lodge was also expanded with an addition and alterations, and part of the added space was dedicated to a cocktail lounge.

To lighten the financial load on skiers, season passes were sold on the installment plan, one-third in the fall, one-third by December 10 and the final one-third by January 10. Adult season passes were $135, teens under 17, $75, and juniors 12 and under, $45. Day rates were increased from $7 to $8, and various packages and multiple-day prices were introduced. Sunday River provided free skiing for schoolchildren who lived in the town of Newry.

A month later, Otten managed to lure Michael Strauss, the *New York Times* ski columnist, to the area, and Strauss told the *Times* readers about the twenty-five-year-old general manager from Teaneck, New Jersey, who drove his car off the road trying to avoid a sanding truck. Strauss quoted Otten as saying, "Nevertheless, we opened on schedule."

The article also told of a new program replacing specialization with integration. This was referred to as snow services, and the program had members of the ski patrol, ski school, lift crew, and snowmaking staff all cross-trained to do each other's jobs. Walker, who was responsible for overseeing the program, said, "That means our personnel can operate on a full scale even at times when some of our key people are not available, possibly through illness."

Each year during this decade as directors came and went, the newest would introduce himself to the volunteer ski patrol and relate how the weekend volunteers would be integrated into this program. It never happened. Whatever the thoughts in the front office, the weekend volunteers had plenty to do on weekends watching out for the safety of the skiers, and the professionals who handled things midweek wound up content to let the weekenders handle their responsibilities on the mountain.

In his 1975 annual report, President Preston Smith told the board of directors, "Sunday River was the first ski area in the State of Maine to open for the season. The ski operations began November 16, 1974, with five inches of machine-made snow on Mixing Bowl. Six days later, we were skiing the full length of the main mountain via the new Ecstasy trail and Lower Cascade. Throughout the season we continued to experience above average conditions until we closed on May 2, 1975, giving us the longest season of any area in Maine of 166 days."

The report went on to explain the increases in revenue and while still operating at a loss, the loss was reduced by 68 percent and the improvement encouraged the parent Sherburne Corporation to purchase an additional $108,000 in common stock. This additional capital was used to exercise land option held by Sunday River. The land was acquired at the base of the area, now occupied by the South Ridge Base area.

The brochure for the 1975–76 season contained the resort's first ski vacation planner complete with packages for lifts, lifts and lessons, and lift, lessons, and equipment. The lodging directory listed the Bethel Spa Motel, Madison Motor Inn in Rumford, Norseman Inn, Philbrook Farm and Shelburne Birches in Shelburne, New Hampshire, Red Rooster Motel, Sudbury Inn, and Sunday River Inn. Adult tickets were $7.50 midweek and $9 weekends and holidays.

The introduction read as follows:

> Remember how it once was?
> Just you and the mountain?
> The "milk run" in the morning, slicing through the quiet and last night's fresh powder?
> Then, somewhere along the way, skiing became big business.
> But not at Sunday River. Up here you'll still find quiet. And friends. Nothing real fancy in the way of night life, but plenty of the simple, unpretentious, good spirit (and the good Yankee cooking) that skiing used to be about.
> You'll find a mile long double chair and a trio of T-bars, plus 14 well-groomed trails with 14 miles of skiing that make you forget your troubles. And, to ensure skiing there's top to bottom snowmaking on both the main mountain and the beginner's slope.
> You'll find our prices on the old fashioned side. For lift tickets. (Is someone complaining?) And Lodging. And ski holiday plans.
> All in all, you'll find skiing as it once was. And still is. At Sunday River in the Great State of Maine.
> It's the best kept ski secret in New England.

The final tag was to be used for some years until skier visit numbers made it clear the secret was out, something that would not happen in the decade of the seventies.

Sunday River kicked off the 1976–77 season with a baked bean supper for season passholders featuring a K2 Aerial Exhibition. An ad for the October 9 event listed Sunday River's season pass price up to that date as $410 for a family of four. An individual adult pass was $155, $175 after that date.

Peter Kailey, general manager of the Sunri Ski Shop and son of Paul Kailey, one of the area founders, coordinated the event, which had the freestyle skiers performing acrobatic maneuvers

The 1975 brochure.

off a special ramp outside the base lodge. The ramp was 40 feet long and 18 feet high. The skiers skied down an Astroturf surface and landed on 20-by-20-foot padded mat. The chairlift operated from noon until 4:00 p.m., giving riders a chance to view the foliage of the western Maine mountains from the top of the mountain without having to climb the 1,500 vertical feet to the summit.

As usual, the early season brought a crisis when a new pump had double the rpm's needed to work properly with the rest of the equipment. The higher speeds would have burned out the bearings, and the only way to operate the system was to use a hand pump to continuously supply the bearings with grease. Les Otten and Burt Mills did this for forty-eight hours straight, sleeping and taking meals in the pump house before turning the task over to other staff members. By documenting everything they did, they finally convinced Ingersol Rand that it was the wrong pump and not the way they were using it. But replacing it would have taken days and the important Christmas season would have been lost without the snowmaking. It was one of many crises that were somehow handled. The skiers never knew how often Sunday River staff worked around the clock so they would have skiing.

The highlight of the season was the biggest ski races in the resort's history. In the February 27 edition of the *Maine Sunday Telegram*, I wrote, "The finest young skiers in the east will be gathering at Sunday River this week to take part in skiing's most demanding event. A total of 140 racers will compete in the Eastern Junior Downhill Championships." At stake were nine places for men and six places for women on the eastern team, which would represent the east in the national championships. The piece went on, "The competitors may be juniors but the course is a real challenge, dropping 1,500 feet over a distance of 8,000 feet. The racers will have to be aggressive from the beginning with a flat to be skated out of the start, followed by an abrupt drop. The next difficult place will be a sharp left turn, a large natural bump and a swing to the right. At that point, the Ecstasy trail flattens out somewhat before a sharp swing to the left onto Lower Sunday Punch. This will be followed by a sharp left and a right turn to the headwall portion of Lower Sunday Punch, one of the steepest parts of the entire mountain. The steepness will provide the greatest speed over the longest straight on the course, setting up for a tight turn to the finish."

"Only the strongest will be able to carry speed through the upper turns and twists and still have the strength to hold their line for the finish. Depending on conditions speeds approaching a mile a minute could be reached on the lower portions of the course. It's the most demanding type of ski racing but the rewards are great for the young skiers."

Somewhere there are records of who won those coveted spots on the eastern team, but they were not available as we put this chronicle together. What we do know is that the event got a lot of attention for Sunday River. A lot of ski areas can host races, but hosting a major downhill, even for juniors, calls for real challenge. In addition, thanks to a team of volunteers from the Sunday River Ski Club, other ski clubs, and the Sunday River staff, the races went off without a hitch. Proving the area could handle this downhill led to the awarding of the Junior Nationals in 1979–80, to close out the decade.

A racer rounds a gate.

Green Berets Find a Skiing Home

When Fred Burk left the U.S. Army in 1965, the former Green Beret had no idea how his association with the army's elite corps would play a key role in a special era for Sunday River and the Special Forces. His first winter after leaving the army, Burk applied his considerable skiing talent as an instructor under Uel Gardner at Sunday River. In the off-season he founded Sunday River Tree Service, operating out of his home on Sunday River Road not far from the ski area.

Unbeknownst to Burk, a former comrade in arms, Special Forces sergeant major David Smith, had been sent on a mission out of Fort Devens in Massachusetts. His quest was to find a suitable place for winter training. He needed to find a place where a full company (two hundred men) could be trained, housed, and fed, and he had a budget for skiing of $12 a day. And it had to be within a reasonable proximity to Fort Devens for travel purposes.

His quest took him from Devens up through Vermont across New Hampshire and up to Sugarloaf and Saddleback in Maine. Still without a decision, he decided once in Maine to look up his friend and headed for Bethel. As Fred Burk recalled, "I had a crew doing some tree work along the highway in Bryant Pond. I was directing traffic and in one of the cars I stopped was Sergeant Major Smith."

The two got together at Burk's place where they talked about the assignment. Burk asked, "What about Sunday River?" They drove up to the mountain where Burk explained what was there, three T-bars, some trails, a base lodge, and a parking lot.

Fred Burk.

Smith asked where the men could be housed and fed, and Burk suggested they take a ride to Rumford to check out the local National Guard armory. The armory would be a perfect place to set up bunks, and the kitchen could be utilized to cook the meals. Sunday River was happy to provide skiing at $12 per day, and why not when their weekend ticket was only $7 at the beginning of the 1971–72 season and this was the summer of 1970.

Records no longer exist to tell us the exact price paid for the Special Forces to ski in the winter of 1970–71, but all who skied that year know it was one of the coldest on record. Over at the Rumford Armory, the Special Forces had been forced to cut wood blocks to protect the drill floor (also used by local schools for basketball) from the steel legs of the bunks.

According to Sergeant Major Smith, the purpose of the training was "the familiarization of military skis and technique, which meant wide track with the ability to

Green Berets get their orders from Commanding General Albin F. Irzyk.

Chapter Three: 1970s

stay on skis while carrying a 70 pound rucksack. The goal was simple. An entire group had to go from point A to point B and arrive together.

It all sounded so simple. But no one had considered two factors, Maine winters and the fact that many of the soldiers had never seen snow, much less temperatures dropping to minus 35 degrees!"

The original plan was to use buses to transport the troops to Sunday River, but the buses were unusable in the cold weather. The only alternative was two-and-a-half-ton trucks, which meant the men would be in the unheated back with their feet on a steel floor. Even the trucks had problems, "The only way to be sure they would run in morning was to keep them running all night." It was so cold that the trucks had to pull over and stop so the men could exercise to warm up. Several stops lengthened the trip, and by the time they arrived at the mountain, all the men could do was head for the base lodge to warm up. Smith recalled, "There was no way we could get them out onto the mountain before they had their hot chocolate and warmed up."

Smith related how the training went, "We had some skiers but most had never seen skis, and some had never seen snow. What we had going for us was superb physical condition, youth and attitude."

The goal of the training was to familiarize the troops with military skis and technique which Smith described as wide track, "At the end of each two week training cycle everyone could negotiate the slopes. We taught sideslip and kick turns, even how to fall onto their backs and lift their skis into the opposite direction."

Wool caps replace the green berets.

Each training cycle was to culminate with a three-day, two-night trip from Gilead, from Evans Notch through the woods to Jackson, New Hampshire. Mostly it was too cold, but late in the season one group made it.

Smith and a small cadre of veteran skiers served as instructors and made pretraining trips to Sunday River to organize how the training would be carried out. He told how the local people opened up their homes and invited them to parties. He cited the Norseman, then operated by Claus and Jacki Wiese, as a place where they were frequent guests. "The people couldn't have been nicer," he said.

One surprise bit of help came when one of the groups arrived in more spectacular fashion. They parachuted into a field off Vernon Street, and Smith told how dozens of snowmobiles were lined up to watch. "Once the men were on the ground, they drove out and gave the men and their equipment a ride to the waiting trucks." As far as he knew, no one had asked the snowmobilers to do this, they just showed up and helped out.

An Associated Press picture of the parachutes with the soldiers suspended below them was captioned "SNOW DRIFT—Green Berets from Fort Devens drift into the drop zone on snow-covered outskirts of Bethel, Me., to begin two weeks of winter training. Men, many of them veterans of service in Southeast Asia, dropped from low flying C-123's into the subzero temperatures of north central Maine. The men were members of the 10th Special Forces in the winter of 1971."

Some of the soldiers embraced the sport, but most simply tolerated it and learned what was necessary to complete the training. One, Master Sergeant Jim Gayer, a World War II veteran, wanted nothing to do with sliding down the mountain on skis. When Sergeant Major Smith demonstrated a stem turn and traverse and directed his group to follow, he turned to watch Gayer "walk down." He had taken peanut butter and jelly from C-rations and coated the bottom of the skis. Smith watched as Gayer lifted each ski with a layer of snow on the bottom in a traverse across the hill where he executed a kick turn and walked to where Smith had stopped.

The Green Berets arrive.

The ski patrol got some extra work, especially on days with fresh snow, which led to frequent falls and some resulted in twisted knees and ankles and an occasional broken bone. But there were benefits, such as having trained medics on station in the ski patrol first aid room. All the patrol had to do was drop off the injured soldier and the medical personnel took over. No one asked what the reaction of recreational skiers was to seeing the U.S. Army ambulance parked outside the aid room every day.

The first year the Special Forces were there (1970–71) the ski patrol still occupied an aid room in the basement of the base lodge, moving into a new building for the 1971–72 season. Not only did their medics help out with injured skiers we brought in, but they were available for other duties as well. When a fire destroyed the lift building at the base of the upper T-bar (T-2), the troops supplied labor to repair the drive and rebuild the building. For two seasons, the Green Berets were an integral part of the ski community at Sunday River.

Green Berets drift into the drop zone.

The Boston House, Party Central

In the late sixties, a group of young professionals from Massachusetts, mostly the Greater Boston area, discovered Sunday River. How the group got organized is unknown. What is known is that they rented a house in Bethel for the winter, the first being on Route 2 partway between the town and Sunday River Road. Another year they occupied the building that is now L'Auberge, and finally one of their numbers bought a place near the fire station. It was a cooperative effort. Each week the menu was decided and the food purchased in Boston. Beer was by the keg (one for twenty people, although I never found out if that was for the weekend or a party). Each person paid so much for the weekend for food and beer.

The ski school and ski patrol had a standing invitation to stop for beer/dinner any Saturday night, but the big blowout always came in February when there would be a huge attendance. We all kicked in for our share and got more than our money's worth. Kegs of beer were stuck in the snowbanks, and when one was emptied the tap was simply moved to another.

Most of the evening was spent with small groups having conversations over food and

A military ambulance for injured soldiers.

beverages, but there was always some kind of game. One year, a game of broom hockey resulted in one broken tailbone and a few other minor injuries. Another year, a racing coach suffered a season-ending knee injury playing Nerf ball soccer, and on one occasion a ski instructor's girlfriend had several ski patrolmen trying to help with her injured knee. The footing provided on loose snow and ice was conducive to injuries.

Perhaps the greatest attention getter was the year of the snow sculpture. Whose idea it was to build a giant phallic symbol is unknown, but it was at least ten feet tall. Had it been behind the house there would have been no problem, but it was on the front lawn, impossible to miss from the road. Members of the group who spent the night told of cars hitting the brakes and backing up to check if what they were seeing was real. It certainly was.

Things hit the fan Monday morning when someone complained to the local police or county sheriff's office. By then all the members of the group had returned to their jobs in Massachusetts, so the police started making calls to find someone connected with the group to take the thing down. They finally located a ski patrolman from South Paris who taught at Oxford Hills. He knew the group, but probably wasn't even at the party. John Parsons was called out of his classroom and asked to tear it down. After classes he drove to Bethel and took care of it.

We called the place the Boston House and have many fond memories of the various members of the group who skied with us (two or three actually patrolled with us) and played as hard as they skied. Although I have some of the names it might be better to leave them anonymous.

Unknown skier and Dave Irons in the mid- to late seventies.

Can Ams and Streaker

The 1975–76 season had a pair of competitive highlights, the 1976 NCAA championships, hosted by Bates College with the jumping and cross-country at Rumford's Chisolm Winter Park and the alpine at Sunday River, and the Canadian American Intercollegiate Alpine Series.

First came the NCAAs with the giant slalom and slalom both run on Lower Cascades. The giant slalom started at the intersection of Bim's Whim and Upper Cascades, while the slalom started just above the spot where skiers cut over from Lower Cascades to Monday Mourning. The trail, with its constant terrain changes, steep pitches, and flatter spots, gave the racers a real challenge and remains one of the most popular race trails on the mountain. The event, which wrapped up with the jumping at Rumford, produced the first tie in the history of the NCAA's when Dartmouth and Colorado wound up with the same number of points. Favored Vermont was third. It was good training for the Can-Ams to follow in late March.

The Can-Ams brought men's and women's teams from NAIA colleges in the United States and Canada for a downhill and two-run giant slalom and slalom races. The local favorite was the University of Maine Farmington team under coach Tom Reynolds. Schools as far away as western Michigan and Ontario came for the racing. Other schools included Harvard, Plymouth State, Johnson State, Lyndon State, Mcgill, Laval, and Dalhousie. Responsibility for organizing the event fell on Sunday River race coach Bob Harkins. Sunri Ski Shop owner Paul Kailey played a key role and brought in Howard Kelton, well-known coach at Middlebury, to set the courses.

For the first time a downhill was set running from the top of Ecstasy, under the upper T-bar, and onto Lower Cascades. Skiers familiar with the mountain can understand the difficulty of the course. After the tight run down Ecstasy with some hard turns, the skiers had a long fall away turn starting at the top of Lower Cascades. Riding the edges hard with the trail falling away to the right, the skiers entered the compression at the top of what is now the lift up from White Cap base. Only the strongest and experienced downhillers were able to keep airtime to a minimum off the big bump coming out of the compression. Those who failed the pre-jump found themselves on the low side as they hit the little headwall, and once again big air was inevitable. It was the site of several crashes, fortunately none involving serious injuries.

A junior racer.

For those of us on ski patrol, this was the cause of one serious glitch. The plan was to start the races every sixty seconds. Unfortunately, that wasn't enough time for the preceding racer to be past that headwall, and one racer actually had to lift one ski to avoid a toboggan removing the racer before him from the course. At that point word was sent to the start to wait until a patroller at the bottom of the headwall called on his radio "Headwall clear" before starting the next racer. The course was relatively tame after that, and those who survived that section were unlikely to find trouble before finishing.

The most interesting incident occurred when a McGill racer crashed at the bottom of the headwall. When our patrolmen approached, he informed them that he was a member of the Canadian National Ski Patrol and he knew his ankle was broken. The force of the crash had blown apart his boot, twisting the cuff in such a way that it was putting great pressure on that ankle, but he insisted no one straighten that boot. The splint was applied around the boot, adding even more pressure, and he was transported in some pain to the aid room. There, the boot was finally removed, bringing immediate relief. The ankle was fine. The displaced boot cuff had caused all the pain. Obviously, the patrol had a chuckle or two over that one. It was also the closest we came to having a real injury that day.

The highlight for many of the racers, at least the ladies, came during their giant slalom. Bob Harkins was the starter and was surprised at the beginning of the race when a guy skied into the start declaring himself a forerunner. Harkins hesitated, but not wanting to hold things up, he said okay and got ready to start. Then the skier took off his parka, revealing a bare chest, and proceeded to take off his warmups, revealing more bare flesh. To the delight of the women gathered at the start he had trouble with the zippers and spent more time in the start than he intended. We suspected something had been arranged when several of the women pulled out cameras.

After a few embarrassing moments he was off, with nothing on but boots, skis, poles, and a helmet. A few of us who had no particular assignments followed him down. At the top of Lower Cascades, he stopped facing a lady gatekeeper and asked, "Did I miss that gate?" Before she could answer he was off. We followed him to the base where he skied through the finish and kept right on going to a spot behind a trailer where clothes were waiting.

It turned out he was from University of Connecticut, and when I talked with the coach after the race he informed me the young man had skied his last race for the university. I told him I could leave the school's name out of my newspaper report if he let the kid stay on the team. I never found out what finally happened, but this is the first place the school is identified. I assume after more than thirty years none of those involved are still with the school.

The races were a great success with the racers liking the terrain and the organization. The weather cooperated with no precipitation from the downhill training to start the event and sunshine on the last two days. The streaker had a warm, sunny day as well. Most of the results are long forgotten, but I do know that Johnson State's Boomer Mumford won all three men's races. Mumford is now a rep for Head ski equipment and still remembers that week very well.

What turned out to be the final season under Sherburne Corporation featured a couple of big events, one New England wide and one at Sunday River. The big New England event was actually a nonevent. It didn't snow. The *Lewiston Daily Sun* on January 17, 1980, ran a front-page story, "The Great Snow Drought," in which it detailed how then governor Brennan was appealing to the SBA for emergency loans for Maine's ski areas. The other was the scheduling for March 1980 of the Junior National Alpines at Sunday River.

Interestingly, the no-snow year got an early boost from an October storm. The October 10th *Portland Press Herald* ran a picture with the caption "Earle Morse, left, an associate coach at Sunday River Ski Area in Bethel, and Alfred Rubins, racing director at the resort, found the skiing on four to six inches of first snow Tuesday to be rough, as Rubins ski pole accumulated some hay on the trip down the mountain." Les Otten was quoted in the piece, "Our company now faces a $130,000 unbudgeted cash drain, with rain predicted tonight. It's all about marketing."

The growth of Sunday River through the eighties actually got a jump start in the no-snow winter. Reports had been running in newspapers throughout New England on the disastrous lack of snow in the mountains, and at Sunday River, Les Otten and his team were trying to figure out how to get the message out that there was snow in the mountains.

Buying ads on Boston TV would not be enough. Something dramatic had to be done. They contacted Bryce Yates, a local logger, and arranged to have one of his dump trucks filled with man-made snow. Yates drove the truck to Boston where ten tons of snow was dumped on the Boston Common. The *Boston Globe* ran a picture the morning of January 4, captioned, "Just to prove there is something to ski on in New England's north country, representatives of the Sunday River resort in Bethel, Maine, frolic in 10 tons of man-made snow trucked to Boston and dumped on the Common yesterday."

This was the beginning of Sunday River's reputation as a ski resort that could always produce good skiing regardless of the weather. Marketing played a key role, but if the skiing product had not been there it would not have worked.

One participant in the show was Dick Rasor, owner of the Bethel Inn Resort. Rasor recalled how they met at the well-known Hill Top Steak House on Route 1 in Saugus to form their vehicles into a convoy to Government Center in Boston. The back seat of Otten's car had been removed to make room for snow guns and hoses. The idea was to dump the snow on the Common while they hooked up to the water system, powered up a generator, and made snow. To get permission and a generator, Otten went into Government Center.

In the meantime, Rasor was with the group dumping the snow. "The police couldn't have been nicer. They directed traffic around us as we tried to dump the snow. Unfortunately, the snow (partially melted by the exhaust under the truck body) had frozen and had to be dug out. It came out in huge frozen chunks which could have crushed someone."

This all happened while Otten was being detained by police trying to explain his lack of a permit. But the results were there. TV crews filmed the event, and it made the evening news. Rasor related, "On the evening news the crawl over the pictures identified me as Sunday River general manager Les Otten."

The event was also being watched up at Killington, and before they could leave town, the officers of the parent Sherburne Corporation called Otten to a meeting at the Hampshire House (home of the Cheers Bar) and informed him that they would take over from there so the Vermont properties could share in the publicity. But Sunday River had already gotten the bulk of the PR, and the press treated claims by other resorts as afterthoughts. That might have been a key event in the rivalry that would build a few years later.

When contacted about the event for this book, Rasor noted, "I can't fathom where the Bethel Inn would be today without Les Otten." That could be said for the entire Bethel area.

Fortunately, it snowed before Sunday River's big event, the National Junior Alpine Championships in mid-March. The competition took place over a week with downhill, giant

Bryce Yates' dump truck being prepared for hauling snow to the Boston Common.

slalom, and slalom titles for men and women. The downhill started near the top of Ecstasy, running the length of that trail and making a sweeping left turn to the top of Lower Sunday Punch and the rest of the course.

The championships received good press coverage and helped Sunday River get the word out for the late season while many areas were closing in late March. As word spread about the resort's ability to make snow and produce good skiing, skier visits grew, and late in the season a column in the *Portland Press Herald* pointed out that Les Otten had reported that ticket sales in the second half of the season had surged 50 percent ahead of the same period for the previous year.

The Three Eras of Les Otten

The story of Sunday River as a ski resort.

The Killington Years

Everyone in the ski business knew about Killington, the giant of Vermont skiing. The resort was only a year older than Sunday River, but thanks to its location in south-central Vermont and the leadership of founder Preston Smith, it was a rare entity, a profitable ski area. Smith's philosophy was simple. It was easier to teach businessmen to ski than to turn skiers into businessmen. He also firmly believed that only by producing a dependable ski product could a ski area survive and prosper. Sound business practices controlled spending, but never at the expense of the quality of the skiing. Killington was one of the very first ski areas to invest heavily in snowmaking and grooming, and it built a reputation as always being the first to open and the last to close.

Les Otten learned his lessons well under its management program, and as the years would show, he added ideas of his own. This was immediately put to work following that first winter. Otten became general manager at the age of twenty-four and took the first steps.

Any increase in skier visits would completely overwhelm the tiny base lodge. Fortunately, Jim Sysko, a graduate engineer, had been brought on to oversee lifts and other operations, and he was the ideal person to design and build an addition that doubled the size of the lodge by extending it toward the slopes for the 1973–74 season.

The following summer in 1974 was the time for a major expansion of snowmaking. By adding top-to-bottom snowmaking, it would be possible to operate the chair in the early season and Sunday River could join the race to be among the first ski areas to open each season. To create an efficient loop, a new trail was cut. Ecstasy ran diagonally across the mountain from the top of the chair to the intersection of trails just above the top of the lower T-bar. By running pipe up Lower Cascades and on up Ecstasy, a continuous top-to-bottom run was created.

When the ski area opened that season, skiers could ride the chair to the summit and enjoy a mile-and-a-half run back to the base. With a few more days of snowmaking Mixing Bowl could

Les Otten.

open, giving Sunday River skiing for novices and intermediates whether it snowed or not.

Top-to-bottom snowmaking was the first step toward expanding the resort and attracting more business, but without more lodging little growth could be expected. A number of places had been built in Viking Village, but they were mostly for season passholders, and rental beds were still well off the mountain. The company set up a forty-five-lot development called Sunday River Village and in 1977, began planning a four-phase condominium project.

Construction of the first phase, South Ridge Condominiums, took place in the summer of 1978 as part of a new base area, with a new lodge adjacent to the units. The Mixing Bowl T-bar was rerouted and extended down to the new base along with snowmaking. A Poma platter lift was installed next to T-1 for additional uphill capacity.

The Vermont Influence

While Les Otten and his team were working to improve things at Sunday River, important changes were taking place in Vermont. One reason for the purchase of Sunday River by Killington was a moratorium in Vermont on ski area expansion. In 1976, that moratorium came to an end and Killington purchased Mount Snow. The focus of the parent company quickly switched from Maine to Vermont as the location of Mount Snow in southern Vermont close to major population centers in New York and Connecticut made more sense for investment.

Through the rest of the seventies, investment at Sunday River trickled almost to a halt. Frustrated with the situation, Les Otten went to Killington and said, in effect, "If you're not going to let me build it up, sell it to me."

Killington management not only agreed, but it financed the $850,000 purchase price, and Otten had a ski area. That set the stage for one of the most explosive growth periods of any ski area.

The trail map in 1978 showing the expanded Mixing Bowl area to the new South Ridge Base Lodge.

Chapter Three: 1970s

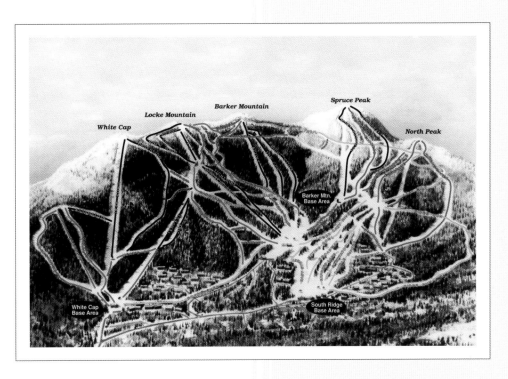

The Eighties and Explosive Growth	69
The Israeli Snow Troops	71
Retail, Chris Otten, and White Heat	73
Entrepreneur of the Year	77
The Sunday River Brand	77
Growth Requires a Banker	79
The Origins of Maine Handicapped Skiing	79
Ski Patrol Reorganizes	83
Sunday River, Do It Yourself Headquarters	84
Looking Back on the Growth Years	84

The Eighties and Explosive Growth

Heading into the 1980–81 season, Les Otten owned Sunday River, but what did he have? The previous season the ski area had attracted only 32,000 skier visits and lost $250,000. Obviously, changes were needed. First he needed a team.

He had Cynthia Mason to handle the books and keep track of the finances, a no-nonsense sharp-eyed bookkeeper. On the mountain he had Burt Mills, a self-taught mechanic who could figure out snowmaking, snowcats, and lift operations. He also had Jim Sysko, an engineer capable of designing buildings, erecting lifts, and setting up snowmaking systems. For marketing and communications he brought in Wende Frutchy (now Wende Gray), who had been director of marketing at Sugarloaf and tried a winter as general manger at the Camden Snowbowl. After a winter with seven straight rainy weekends at the coastal ski area she was ready to return to the western Maine mountains, and Otten had his team in place.

That winter they cut the loss to $80,000 and in 1981–82 earned a profit of $135,000. That set the trend for the eighties, but it wasn't easy.

Otten laid out his ideas with direct simplicity. "First you have to get skiers, you have to teach people how to ski and steal skiers from other areas. To do this you have to have a better product. Once you get them you have to retain them and house them."

It all added up to improving snowmaking and grooming, upgrading lifts, and creating lodging. Looking at the mistakes of other resorts that had built six-figure homes on large lots, he realized that this didn't sell lift tickets. Skiers who could afford such homes didn't need the rental income, so he designed inexpensive condos that attracted buyers who needed the rental income, which would give him the needed bed base. Early units sold for as little as $28,500. As Otten once summed it up, "For every one who can afford a $100,000 unit there are a thousand who could stretch to buy one for $50,000."

With those ideas, Sunday River was on the move. But it needed capital. One of the first needs was a learning area friendlier to new skiers. That meant a chairlift was needed for Mixing Bowl and a base lodge at South Ridge where they could rent equipment and go directly to the beginner runs.

In order to build a chairlift that summer of 1981, Otten turned to "Rugged" Chapman, a local junk dealer. Scouring the mountain and buildings, employees gathered up every loose piece of copper, iron, and aluminum, which was then sold to Chapman. The last lots in Viking

Marketing director Wende Gray sneaks out of the office to check snow conditions.

Village were sold, and thirty lifetime passes at $1,500 each. A total of $90,000 was raised, and an SBA loan took care of the rest. For the 1981–82 season new skiers rode a double chairlift and skier visits increased to 50,000.

Although six new townhouses were added at South Ridge, and an additional base building was constructed at South Ridge, the biggest news in 1982 was the creation of Maine Handicapped Skiing.

Another key piece of the Otten strategy was getting the word out. A limited advertising budget restricted that avenue, so it was decided to pursue the press to have ski writers spread the word. One organization, the Eastern Ski Writers Association (ESWA), had more than 150 members scattered throughout the east, writing for magazines and newspapers of all sizes. The organization met monthly through the ski season starting in December. That first meeting was always a crap shoot, especially in the days of limited snowmaking, and 1982 was one of the worst. After a brief window of good snowmaking weather, temperatures climbed. Only a handful of ski areas had any skiing at all, and at Killington, famous as the first to open and last to close, skiers had to walk from one patch of snow to the next to continue their run. Sunday River had one continuous run from the top of Mixing Bowl to the bottom.

Wende Gray remembered advertising "the only continuous run in New England." That first Saturday in December, with dozens of ski writers hitting the lift, temperatures climbed into the sixties. After a few runs under the bright sun, I remember being drenched in perspiration even though dressed only in stretch pants and a turtleneck.

Ski school director Anne Friedlander gets behind her student.

The risky strategy worked. The writers returned to their homes and wrote about the fun they had skiing in almost summerlike temperatures. They wrote about how well the man-made snow held up to the warmth. The late Bob Triplett wrote in his ski column in one of Boston's North Shore weeklies, "So this column is being written in praise of man-made snow . . . without which I and 100 or so others would have been faced with a dull and boring weekend. As it turned out, we all had a happy time on the two trails that Sunday River had been covering with the stuff. The surface was fast and skiable, corning nicely as the day wore on and the temperatures rose."

Triplett went on to explain how the area would have had a lot more skiing terrain open had not the temperature hit one of the highest levels ever recorded in Maine in December. His sentiments were echoed in a number of other publications, and Sunday River had taken another important step in its growing reputation for snowmaking prowess.

The Israeli Snow Troops

One highlight of the ESWA meeting was the banquet Saturday night at the Bethel Inn. Owner Dick Rasor had brought in his brother as an after-dinner speaker. Appearing in full uniform, Bill Rasor was introduced as a general in the Israeli army, head of the ski troops. At his side was Maureen, his assistant, also in full uniform. Bill Rasor went on to detail the training of his ski troops and their expertise at winter warfare. A few of the writers were completely taken in by the spoof, one in particular, Craig Altschul, president of the group at that time.

A special offered a group ski lesson, lift ticket, and rental equipment for $10. Lift tickets were $12 midweek and $16 weekends. A preseason press release listed the mountain stats:

Elevation: 2,630 feet, Vertical Drop 1,630 feet
   Lifts 2 Double Chairlifts—Lift Capacity: 3,800 skiers per hour
   2 T-bars
   1 Poma

Trails: 21 trails (20% advanced, 45% intermediate, 35% novice), FIS approved downhill course, 3 mile novice trail from top.

Snowmaking:
70 acres, top to bottom coverage for all skiing ability levels with 50% of the skiing terrain covered by snowmaking, air/water system.

Area Personnel:
President and General Manager	Leslie B. Otten
Operations Manager	Burt Mills
Marketing Manager	Wende Gray
Vice President and Office Manager	Christine B. Otten
Ski Patrol Supervisor	David Corliss
Ski School Director	Ann Friedlander
Condominium Rental and Property Manager	Lee Randlett
Public Relations Director	Rich Kent

Skier visits for 1982–83 hit 65,000.

The next summer added more beds with the first wing of the Cascades Condominiums and the center core of the building uphill from the South Ridge Base Lodge. In order to accommodate the growing number of skiers and to keep things rolling when the aging Pullman Berry lift was down, the Locke Mountain triple was installed. This made possible the retirement of T-2, and the former lift line was widened for a new run appropriately named T-2.

In the early eighties Ski New England was a marketing group for several of the biggest ski resorts in the six states, and Sunday River insisted on membership; as Wende Gray put it, "We faked being in the big leagues."

It was one thing to fake being in the big leagues. It was another to go head to head and proclaim superiority. Sunday River took its own survey and cherry picked the results to show how it was better than the competition. According to the survey by a "major ski area consulting firm," responding skiers compared Sunday River with the ski area they had previously skied most often and rated Sunday River better overall in categories of lift lines, grooming, fun to ski, and value for the dollar. The competition cried foul, but that only drew more attention to the survey. The one key area that Sunday River wanted to put out was the area's ability to make snow, to recover faster than any other ski area following a thaw. Gray noted, "We always did best in the worst of times."

When things were bad around the region, Sunday River's reputation for making snow regardless of the weather brought skiers from all over. In Otten's words, "We could turn on a dime." Skier visits jumped to 88,000 on the twenty-fifth anniversary in December 1984.

In 1984, another thirty-six-unit wing was added to Cascades Condominiums, doubling that cluster, and Sunrise Condominiums were erected, adding another sixty-four units. The Barker Lodge was doubled in size, and another building was added to the South Ridge base. To fill the new beds and added lodge space, Sunday River introduced the first Learn to Ski in One Day program and guaranteed the results.

This was part of Les Otten's idea that in order to succeed new skiers had to be created. Skiers could be stolen from other ski areas, but that was a limited resource. The pie had to be expanded, not just divided differently. The guarantee was fairly simple. Nonskiers could sign up for a lesson and an instructor would stay with them for the entire day if necessary, making sure they could successfully negotiate the beginner slopes by the end of the day. If, on that rare occasion, a new skier simply couldn't manage the skills, a full refund was available.

It was a great marketing tool, but what it led to was the key to Sunday River using ski school to build the sport. The next step was "ski all you can see." One of the biggest problems with skiing has always been retaining skiers, even to the point where skiers would take one lesson and never return. A way had to be found to lock these skiers in.

Recognizing that while a newbie could develop sufficient skills to ski the beginner slopes in a day but it takes a series of lessons and practice to ski from the top of the mountain, a plan was devised to encourage an early commitment. On the day of the first lesson, skiers were shown a

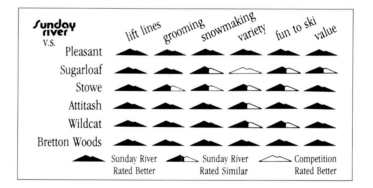

The chart that stirred up the competition.

video introduction to skiing that explained how skiers developed the skills to ski all they could see as they looked up at the mountain.

They were offered an option of expanding their commitment from a single lesson to three, and those completing the program could purchase a special ski package from Rossignol, skis, bindings, and poles for $195.

To make all this work, a segregated learning center was built at South Ridge. New skiers were carefully led from sign up to rentals and onto the slopes without hassle. Once identified as newcomers, everything was done for them with someone always at hand to guide them. The program worked extremely well, and the ski school grew to accommodate the increased business. It set the stage for another revolution in ski instruction a few years later. Skier visits totalled 125,000.

Retail, Chris Otten, and White Heat

When Chris Otten accompanied her husband to Sunday River in 1972, she was immediately pressed into service running the cafeteria for the first two winters. After that she took a hiatus to raise children at least to the point where they would go off to school. When the youngest reached the age of five and was heading off to school in the fall of 1984, she started a new career. Taking a sales and marketing course over the winter, she went to the spring shows in 1984, and that fall she opened Chris Sports.

"Betsey Paquette and I ran the shop that first year and we put $30,000 on the bottom line," she related. "Of course we didn't pay any rent or utilities but Les said, 'Hey it's one third of a Pisten Bully.'"

At that time the shop was strictly soft goods, and the following year was a good snow year. Sales for 1985–86 tripled. A shop was added at Barker, and hard goods were added. Chris pointed out that she had a boss who let her do her own thing.

Following the very successful season of 1984–85, the first major expansion to another peak took place when the North Peak triple was installed along with the Fall Line double. This added approximately forty acres of trails and meshed with the new Fall Line Condominiums where the north and west wings added sixty-four units of ski-in/ski-out lodging. Twelve more South Ridge Townhouses went in and the first eight units of the Merrill Brook Condominiums.

An important precedent was set when all the new terrain had snowmaking, increasing the total capacity by 50 percent. This fit Les Otten's philosophy of always guaranteeing the skiing product. Henceforth, every expansion would have equal parts trails, uphill capacity, snowmaking, and grooming. At the same time, the separate buildings at South Ridge were connected to create one large base lodge. Retaining skiers was also addressed with the resort's first frequent-skier program.

The new trail map listed two triple chairs, three double chairs, and a T-bar, and the bright yellow designating snowmaking covered more trails than not. Lift tickets were $17 midweek and $22 on weekends. Skier visits totalled 183,000.

Expansion continued in the summer of 1986 with two triple chairlifts and another peak.

The brochure tells the whole story of the Learn to Ski in One Day program.

One lift carried skiers out of South Ridge to a point high enough to access the other at the base of Spruce Peak. Trail acreage was boosted by fifty acres, all with snowmaking, giving the mountain a total of 80 percent snowmaking coverage. New compressors were brought in to ensure plenty of power for the new guns. To house the expected increase in skiers, the south and east wings of the Fall Line Condominiums added sixty-four units. Merrill Brook II added eight units, thirty-six units were added at South Ridge, and North Peak I and II added seventy-two more. They proved to be needed as skier visits leaped to 244,000.

The 1986–87 season came to an abrupt end when a combination of rain and melting snow raised the brooks running off the mountain and the Sunday River. The resulting floods on April Fool's Day cut off Sunday River Road, actually stranding people who lived on the mountain and further on Sunday River Road. The Androscoggin also came up, cutting off both Routes 2 and 26 near Bethel. Extensive roadwork had to be done to several roads in the area, including the Sunday River Road.

Joe Aloisio arrived to take over as engineering manager that summer of 1987, and as he recalled, "I never got in the door." Les Otten and Bill Shanahan (director of development) were coming out and Les said to Bill, "Let's take our engineer." They drove to Augusta and bought the land for Jordan Bowl from International Paper. When Aloisio saw all the plans for lifts trails and buildings, he knew this would be no temporary position, and he is still there twenty-one years later.

A pair of lifts highlighted that summer of 1987. The most popular was the Sunday River Express, a detachable quad that replaced the original Pullman Berry double, finally eliminating the various problems caused by that prototype lift and giving skiers a quick trip to the top where two new advanced runs, Top Gun and Right Stuff, brought new challenges. The other lift, a fixed-grip quad, gave skiers staying in the Brookside Condominiums a direct ride to the midpoint of Lower Cascades, exiting onto that run at the intersection of Cascades Cutoff. The lift started near a local watering hole, D. W. McKeen's, a popular nightspot, and extended the vertical of the mountain.

Expansions during the summer of 1988 yielded results in two ways. Skiers got more terrain, lifts, and lodging, and Sunday River was able to make a big splash in the press. The cutting of White Heat was the most dramatic trail addition to date. It was ballyhooed as the "steepest longest widest" lift-served trail in the east, a claim that produced plenty of arguments from other ski resorts.

The new trail was introduced at a New York press conference where Wende Gray handed out protractors so all the writers could see the exact pitch of White Heat. Otten said to the gathering, "It's not the longest and it's not the steepest and it's not the widest, but it is the longest-steepest-widest."

The marketing success of the expansion was evident when skier visits for the 1988–89 season increased by over 100,000 to a total of 350,000. With those results, the marketing department at Sunday River was happy to have a raging debate in the press about whether its claims of "steepest longest widest" were accurate. For the record, I never used those words in anything I wrote or broadcast.

The big debate actually obscured somewhat just how big an expansion Sunday River achieved that summer. A new base lodge, White Cap, was built, and a pair of fixed-grip quad lifts were installed, one traveling out of the new base area to a point to the east and above the new lift up the right side of White Heat. A total of fifty acres of trails were added, all with snowmaking. Additional compressors and pumps were brought on line, and coverage expanded to 90 percent. A pressure-controlled snowmaking system was also conceived.

More lodging was created with the first twenty-eight units in White Cap Building A and the first eight Locke Mountain Townhouse units opened. This expansion also benefited the thirty-plus owners of property in the area's first real estate development. When Road Runner, a trail from Barker Base to White Cap, was cut to accommodate the Locke Mountain Townhouses, skiers in Viking Village were able to simply walk across the access road and ski down to a lift. Twenty-two years after the first lots were sold, the residents of Viking Village had ski-in/ski-out lodging. Prices in the village immediately escalated, and today the forty or so places in Viking Village are highly prized.

Naturally, various ways to use the new steep run to get press about the ski resort were developed. The ski patrol was recruited for one effort, and the White Heat Toboggan Challenge was born. Ski patrols were invited to send teams of three to the competition, which would be contested on the new run. The rules were simple.

From a start near the top of the trail, the toboggans operated by a skier between the handles in front, another as a passenger, and a third helping control the descent with a tail rope had to follow a course down through the moguls on the right side of the run. The fastest time won.

Ski patrols from as far away as New York and Canada sent teams, and even though the event took place midweek, it always drew a bunch of skiers to watch the challenge. The competition didn't replicate a ski patrol certification exam. During those exams patrollers are expected to pick the smoothest route, giving the passenger an easy ride to the base. Gates force the teams through the steepest, meanest bumps, and the running clock calls for speeds far greater than any on-duty patroller would ever hit with an injured passenger.

Successful runs were the exception. Falls by the front driver were frequent, and passengers falling out were common occurrences. Over the years one team had the most success, and the unique trophy often found a home at Sugarloaf. The theme of the event was based on sled dogs, a term often applied to patrollers. "If you ain't the lead dog, the scenery never changes." The trophy was a handsome oak plaque on which was mounted under clear plastic a full-color photograph of the rear end of a husky with his tail raised.

Another event was created to showcase White Heat and to boost ticket sales in the spring. The first Bust n' Burn competition took place the first weekend in April, inviting local skiers to thrash through the bumps on the new steep run. Bill Jensen remembered how he had just started and the marketing department ran the event with about fifty participants. "It was supposed to have some energy but came across as small time and pretty modest."

After such a flurry of activity, 1989 was fairly quiet, but the season was eventful. The east's first lift-served mountain bike program was introduced in an effort to boost summer business. On the mountain, a halfpipe was built on Lower Tempest near the White Cap base, and initial tests were performed on the pressure-controlled snowmaking system. A new direction in lodging made two hundred beds available for as little as $20 per night when the Snow Cap Ski Dorm opened. More condo units came on line with the opening of White Cap Building B.

Early promotion for White Heat.

A skier throws a daffy in one of the first Bust n' Burn mogul competitions.

The trophy for the White Heat Toboggan Challenge is inscribed, "If you ain't the lead dog, the view never changes."

Entrepreneur of the Year

At the end of the 1988–89 season, skier visits were ten times what they had been when Les Otten bought the resort in 1980. For his turnaround of Sunday River, he was recognized by *Inc. Magazine* as "Entrepreneur of the Year for 1989." My column in the *Lewiston Sun Journal* reported how Otten had increased skiing acreage from seventy to more than four hundred, added nine new chairlifts, and tripled base facilities, and even more important to the local economy increased year-round employment to 150 and seasonal to 500. And most of the growth had been self-financed through profits and real estate sales.

Speaking at an Eggs and Issues breakfast in Portland, when asked to reveal his formula, Les Otten responded, "Set a goal and work your tail off."

The Sunday River Brand

Sometimes a mishap can have a much larger impact than appears at the time. After two years as patrol director, Skip King had moved into mountain operations. The summer Right Stuff and Top Gun were cut, King headed down Right Stuff on an ATV. Not realizing the machine had to be started downhill in first gear, he tried to downshift. When it didn't work and as the machine sped out of control, he was forced to jump. He landed on his radio, and the injuries kept him off the hill the rest of that summer.

That moved him into public relations and communications, where he would work until 2002, first for Sunday River and finally for the American Skiing Company (ASC). One of his first introductions to marketing was accompanying Otten to produce some video. Realizing his background in theater gave him the tools to handle the radio and TV feeds, he was soon assigned these tasks.

At the time in the early nineties, if one had asked a staff member to identify the Sunday River brand, no one could have. What Sunday River was doing had started in the eighties. Simply put, the resort was the upstart kid, stepping in to compete against the big boys. Otten had figured out that snow reporting and snow phones were the single most important part of the daily marketing of a ski area. King took that to the next level.

Doing daily radio feeds, King became a character, cheeky, in your face, fitting what was going on at the resort at the time. It was a likeable character that actually branded Sunday River without knowing it.

To take advantage of the immediacy of radio and the visual impact of TV, they had a full-on TV and recording suite at the mountain. King would write, produce, and transmit six spots daily to various radio stations. The company purchased a Cessna 172 and took aerial shots of the mountain. Within forty-five minutes they could do a voice-over and have a TV spot ready to transmit.

Skip King was the most recognized name associated with Sunday River, after Otten. Many businessmen had the name "Skip" on speed dials to identify the resort snow phones. By the end of the nineties the resort was attracting 550,000 skier visits and could hardly be called an upstart kid, but the brand had worked. Sunday River was now the headquarters for a multiresort conglomerate, having outgrown many of its rivals, and even acquiring several of them.

The big event of the winter of 1989–90 was the first Legends of Freestyle added to Bust n' Burn. Once again utilizing the bumps on White Heat, this event celebrated the original freestyle skiers, a group known for breaking new ground. Scott Brooksbank and Wayne Wong led the parade, and Sunday River skiers got to watch some of the best bump skiers ever demonstrate their skills. Regular recreational skiers who struggled with such bumps, or skied them slowly and carefully, could only look on with envy as these skiers made it all look easy.

These were the heroes of the seventies. Deno Dudenake and John Clendenon were there along with others who had thrilled crowds of skiers as they toured, swiveling through the bumps and grabbing air two or three times on each run. The idea of bringing them to Sunday River came from then vice president of marketing, Bill Jensen. He went out on a limb, betting the budget of $42,000 that it would pay off in publicity and drawing skiers who wanted to ski the same challenging White Heat where the legends competed.

Hot air balloons rise above the South Ridge base area.

Mogul champion Deno Dudenake proved he still had it, skiing away with the first prize of $2,500. The event paid off for the top eight with number eight getting $250. But it wasn't the prize money that the freestyle legends appreciated most. Dudenake remembered, "They really rolled out the red carpet for us. They put us up and wined and dined us for all three days."

Jensen recalled later, "Until Saturday morning at 9:00 a.m. I did not know if this bet (my bet with Les's money) would be one of the best days in Sunday River's history or my last day. Fortunately for me the bet paid off big time."

At the time, Sunday River was out to promote White Heat and Bust n' Burn over Killington's Outer Limits and their bump competition. For the record, the bet paid off with 6,000 skiers each day and close to $500,000 in revenue. Not only was it huge financial success but the event was a breakout moment for Sunday River, proving it could host and promote a truly world-class ski event.

The late I. William Berry, one of the most recognized ski writers and editors ever, used the event to introduce an article in *Ski World* outlining the success of Otten and Sunday River in which he labeled Otten as "King of the Ski Moguls."

The skiers at the event had another key impact. Les Otten was watching the crowd at Bust n' Burn and saw skiers hungry for skills. These were terminal intermediates gaping at higher skills, and they were envious. Otten figured these skiers probably skied five days a year but

Bankers Roger Conant and Jim Delamater with Les Otten and his kids, Meredith and BJ, and Ed Vachon.

Maine Handicapped Skiing's first student. Kim Salzmann with instructor Dannie Force.

would ski more if they skied better. If he could get them up to six days a year that would be a 20 percent increase. The question was how to get them into ski school where they could enhance their skill levels.

The event wrapped up the eighties and another record year with 395,000 visits. It set the stage for growth continuing into the nineties.

Growth Requires a Banker

No program of growth can take place without a bank or two, and Sunday River was no different. Jim Delamater, then president of Bethel Savings Bank, recalled first meeting Les Otten in 1981. He asked Otten if he had a business plan. "Les took me into his office and showed me his plan, for two years, five years, seven years and beyond. He had the maps on the wall showing 25 years of growth."

Delamater told how they needed to presell the units. At the time the bank was a "tiny" company, but he was sold on Otten's plans and agreed to buy units so that a larger bank would approve going forward with the next phase. That fall one of his loan officers, Mary Ann Brown, coordinated a day of closings. All thirty-six units were closed right there on the mountain in a single day. Delamater praised the real estate sales team at the mountain, his staff at the bank, and all concerned. "It was exciting. The papers were being signed as furniture was coming in."

It was the second time Bethel Savings played a key role in Sunday River. In the very beginning its president was Ed Vachon, who had helped the ski area get started in 1959. Through the eighties, the partnership continued. Both the resort and the bank grew. Bethel Savings acquired other banks and in 1987 went public, becoming Northeast Bank in 1994. Jim Delamater is president and CEO today.

The Origins of Maine Handicapped Skiing

The story actually got its start during an annual ritual with the family of Klaus and Beverly Salzmann in the fall of 1979. Each year this family of Sunday River skiers dragged out the ski boots so the boys, Craig and Kirk, could try them on and see who needed new gear for the coming season. Their baby sister, Kim, who suffered with cerebral palsy, had been left out of the family sport, but on this occasion she wanted to join the fun and try on ski boots. Her older brothers obliged and buckled her feet into a pair of boots.

With her condition, Kim had never been able to walk, but once helped to her feet, the stability of the ski boots allowed her to stand and walk! Klaus and Beverly asked each other, "If she can walk, why not ski?" Beverly recalled, "Klaus ran down to Steve Wight's (the Sunday River Inn and Cross Country Ski Center) and got some of those little fish scale skis." The next step was actually getting Kim on skis, and that took place at Sunday River where the family had a ski home. During Christmas vacation in 1979, with her father, Klaus, as her instructor,

Kim made her first ski runs on the South Ridge beginner slopes. A ski bra (a device used to lock the ski tips together) was used to aid in controlling the skis.

Out on the beginner slope, Kim would manage about ten feet and fall, but she loved it. Klaus skied behind holding her between his legs. Then he cajoled the ski school to work with her. They took an immediate interest, and Kim was on her way.

Later that season, Beverly Salzmann told her daughter's orthopedist about Kim being able to walk and ski due to the stability provided by the ski boots. Dr. Omar "Chip" Crothers insisted she bring the boots in on their next appointment so he could see for himself. A short time after that, Crothers, also an avid skier, got to watch Kim in action, "I saw her ski, not running gates, but skiing and having fun."

"I was doing a lot of children's orthopedics and I had an idea," he continued. In discussing his idea with a friend, he learned that a disabled ski program already existed at Winter Park Resort, the Colorado ski area owned by the City of Denver. He called Hal O'Leary, the former ski instructor who had started and ran that program. Dr. Crothers recalled how O'Leary had told him, "I don't want to talk to you until you can tell me you have a ski area willing to accommodate a program."

That led to a letter to Les Otten, and after an exchange of letters and a discussion Otten agreed to have a handicapped skiing program. When he again contacted O'Leary he felt that the National Sports Center for the Disabled (NSCD) director was surprised to hear from him, figuring he would not find an area and would simply disappear. O'Leary said, "Find someone who understands disabilities and can ski, not an instructor."

Crothers found Meredith Elcombe, a physical therapist at the Maine Medical Center. Elcombe remembered his approach, "How would you like to go to Winter Park and NSCD for three weeks?"

She headed for Colorado, where the folks at Winter Park included her in their program from mid-November through Thanksgiving. "It was invaluable," she said.

Elcombe recalled how Dr. Crothers had talked Maine Medical Center into allowing her a four-day workweek so she could spend a day each week working with five students in the first year of Maine Handicapped Skiing. By the end of the first year, there were eight students in the program, including Kim. At the end of the year they began gathering volunteers and initiated a training program to teach them how to work with the handicapped.

With the help of Sunday River staff, Elcombe learned how to fit boots and set up rental skis. The first equipment for the handicapped was ski bras and outriggers, ski poles with hinged skis in place of baskets. Entering its second year in 1983, the program had Elcombe as full-time director, a number of volunteer instructors, and enough equipment for thirty skiers.

Both Elcombe and Crothers credited ski school director Anne Friedlander as playing a key role, along with Nat Putnam, another instructor.

In the early years, Maine Handicapped Skiing operated out of various spaces, one year in the basement at South Ridge and another next to the rental shop. In 1987, Paula Berry (now Wheeler), who had worked for Sunday River under Wende Gray, became executive director, and her energy and dedication played a key role in the growth of the program. While working in the resort's marketing department she had also played a major role in 1986 when the first

Ski-A-Thon was held. This event with teams of skiers riding the Locke Mountain triple to make as many runs as they could to raise money for the program was a huge success from that first day. Each team had gathered pledges of so much per run. (The wiser competitors, including myself, found out what the maximum was each donor would contribute and set the amount per run according to what they felt they could comfortably complete.) Our team led by Les Otten won the event with $9,000 raised by five or six skiers. That inaugural Ski-A-Thon raised a total of $38,000.

In 1991, Maine Handicapped Skiing moved into a new building on land donated by Sunday River and Les Otten adjacent to the beginner slope. This allowed the program's students to change away from the bustle of the base lodge and ski directly onto the slopes.

Betsey Doyon, executive director from 1992–2008, said the Ski-A-Thon is still the single-biggest fundraiser for the organization, which also runs a fall appeal, applies for grants, and has corporate sponsors and individual donors. The Ski-A-Thon now raises in excess of $300,000 annually with a high of $325,000 in 2006.

From eight students the first season, Maine Handicapped Skiing now has 250 students each winter and 80 in summer. There is some doubling up, so Doyon estimates the total to be 285–290. Where there were mostly children in the beginning, the majority are now adults, as victims of injuries and strokes use the program as part of rehabilitation. Also taking part were Iraq veterans returning with disabilities. During the 2007–2008 season Northeast Mobile Health Services provided a bus once a week from Portland at a minimal charge so Maine Handicapped Skiing could offer free transportation to at least some of the participants. And that brings up an important feature of the program. From the very first day it has been totally free to the students, including instruction, equipment, and lift tickets.

Kim Salzmann takes the skills learned in Maine Handicapped Skiing abroad.

Over four hundred volunteers teach, assist with equipment fitting, drive snowmobiles, and even carpool to assist students who need transportation. In addition, the program has been expanded to Sugarloaf, the Sunday River Inn, and the Pineland Center.

Meredith Elcombe summed up the feelings of Doyon and Crothers as well as herself, "You get a reward of vicariously feeling the accomplishments of the students, especially when one comes to you and says, 'You don't know what this means to me. Before skiing I was down and out. Now I feel very special.'" All agreed that it was heartwarming to see families and volunteers become family.

And what of that little girl who started it all? Kim Salzmann traveled to Europe when her father's company transferred him to Munich and got to ski in the Alps at such renowned resorts as St. Anton. She completed college and has been working for IBM in Burlington, Vermont, for seven years. She still loves to ski.

Ski Patrol Reorganizes

In 1987, Skip King was brought in as patrol director. After a number of years as a professional patrolman at Killington, his job was to reorganize the ski patrol at Sunday River. King saw three things that needed to be addressed. He wanted the volunteers and professionals to work together as a team, and to that end he immediately dressed all members in the same parkas. Next he set up procedures and training that assured all members met the same standards. Trail logs were instituted to be sure that as patrollers took runs all the trails were skied, allowing a more thorough knowledge of conditions around the mountain.

The addition of White Heat before the 1988–89 season added another dimension to patrol skills needed. Up until that time, most of Sunday River's runs were intermediate with some advanced pitches. Agony was left to mogul up, and Top Gun and Right Stuff had some steeps, but nothing compared to the sustained steeps of White Heat. This placed a new emphasis on toboggan training. Controlling a rescue toboggan on such pitches called for a high level of skill and strength, and training was increased to answer the demand.

After three years, Skip King felt he had met most of the needs and accepted a new challenge as communications director for the resort at a time when Sunday River was entering into a pitched battle with Maine's other giant ski resort, Sugarloaf.

The job of patrol director fell to Chip Seamans, who had been a seasonal patrolman for six years, a job he held until moving on to become an assistant to mountain manager Burt Mills. When Mills took on the role of directing operations at the acquisitions for ASC, Seamans moved up to mountain manager and in 1998 became general manager for the resort.

Tim Bruce, who had joined the patrol under Skip King as a regular patrolman, succeeded Seamans as patrol director in 1997 and served through 2004. In 2003, risk management was added to his patrol director duties, and in 2004, he became risk manager full time. When he left Outward Bound he didn't envision nineteen years at Sunday River. He described some of the misconceptions about ski patrolling. One is that the core is the professional. While there is a professional director and there are usually a handful of pros who return each year, he pointed out that there is always a turnover among the pros. The volunteers tend to return year after year and can be counted on to provide a high level of competence on weekends and holidays.

It's quite a contrast from the days when Donald Angevine was concerned about having to cover Lazy River when T-2 was installed, or even when I had to be concerned about covering the top of T-2 and the Barker Double. As the fiftieth anniversary of Sunday River approaches, the resort operates with twenty to twenty-five paid patrollers and fifty volunteers, all equipped with radios. During operating hours patrollers are stationed at the top of White Cap, Barker, Spruce, and Jordan.

A number of them are emergency medical technicians, but Bruce says the outdoor emergency care course is fine. Through his nineteen years he has seen improvements in hill maintenance and communication between departments, along with a continuing emphasis on training. He shoots down the romance of the job when he points out that patrollers spend a high percentage of their time skiing without poles, that they are often "janitors on skis."

Now that he is no longer actively patrolling, Bruce says he misses the energy of starting up in the fall but not the take down in the spring, a real pain. On the subject of after-hour searches for lost children, he notes that it's usually a case of the family simply being separated, "The kids are fine, the parents are lost."

Sunday River, Do It Yourself Headquarters

The growth of the eighties was unique in a number of ways, but perhaps the most significant was that it was achieved without massive debt and the company made profits each year even while investing heavily in lifts, snowmaking, trails, lodging, and infrastructure. Les Otten revealed the secret when he told how he and Burt Mills once spent thirty-six straight hours getting pumps to work and thawing pipes. "There wasn't a job that management wouldn't do."

He pointed out how they learned to run a transit to survey and lay out Sunday River Village. "We didn't contract out. We had our own woodworking shop, sent employees to welding school and had others trained as crane operators. We kept everybody employed."

Otten related how Mills had laid out the "best" compressor building, and how used oil was burned to heat the floor of the garage so workers could work in T-shirts. By the end of the decade Sunday River's lodging had expanded from 18 units to 460 units of varying sizes, along with the 200-bed Snow Cap Ski Dorm, and skier visits had grown from 32,000 to 395,000.

Value lodging, the Snow Cap Ski Dorm.

Looking Back on the Growth Years

Of all the growth in the eighties, four years were the busiest in terms of expansion. Jay Gamble, who was in charge of lift operations, parking, ski patrol, lift construction, civil works, concrete for lift tower bases, trails, and snowmaking, recalled some of the challenges that came with building eight lifts, two each year for four years. "In several of these chairlift locations such as North Peak, Spruce Peak, Little White Cap, White Heat, Whitecap, Aurora and Quantum Leap, almost the entire trail network was constructed in the same summer. That including trail cutting, drilling and blasting, grading slopes stabilization and snowmaking installation."

Once the tower foundations were in place, and Gamble was laying pipe for snowmaking, Dan

Another lift on the ground and through the air.

Lift foundation being poured.

Wheeler, whose winter job was keeping all things mechanical running properly, was watching over helicopters as they set towers, stringing cable and installing the electrical systems for the lifts. Wheeler remembered well the crisis of the failed load test of the Oz chair, "I told Les we had to have his plane to go for parts. By having the parts flown in we got the lift ready for a new test in just 36 hours."

He also recalled how they lost the motor on one lift Christmas week in 1988. When told they couldn't repair the motor, that it would have to be shipped to Texas for factory repairs, Wheeler, took the drawings of the motor and figured out how to remove and repair the bearings on site, still in the lift's engine room, salvaging the vacation.

Gamble related the difficulties encountered in building a trail on terrain as steep as White Heat, "We had to devise a way to control bull dozers and other equipment to move rocks and earth. I designed pins made of inch and a half steel and ordered them from Isaacson Steel in Berlin, NH. We drilled holes four feet into the granite so we could winch the equipment down. New holes had to be drilled and the pins reset every day as the equipment moved down and across the slope."

The huge boulders were drilled and blasted down to manageable size, then 100 bales of hay were dropped from a helicopter 200 feet above the trail. The bales burst on contact and filled in the crevices in the broken rock. More hay was stuffed in between the rocks by hand and combined with the meager amount of topsoil on the mostly granite run, they were able to grow grass the following summer.

The eighties were extraordinary years, especially the four years when eight new lifts went in along with trails, snowmaking, and lodging enough to accommodate the new skiers attracted. During that period skier visits increased from 125,000 in the middle of the decade to 395,000 at the end.

Burt Mills as mountain manager had to make sure existing lifts, trails, snowmaking, and other equipment was ready for the winter along with the new stuff. Wheeler recalled Otten telling him at the beginning of this intensive expansion, "It will be like an out of control locomotive. Just hang on."

Naturally, during our conversations plenty of memories came back for both of us. One was an individual we both knew well. Bernie Powers sat at the top of the Barker double for many years, all through the seventies and into the eighties. He never road that lift without his "ammo box" (one of those steel boxes used by the military to carry ammunition). What Burt Mills didn't know for some time was that the box contained enough rope for Bernie to lower himself out of the chair. He had been stranded for a time once when the lift broke down and he didn't trust it. As with all lift attendants he would ride down after the lifts were closed and he didn't want to spend the night. Wheeler remembered when he learned about the rope. What he didn't know was that everyone on the patrol who spent time on shifts in the shack with Bernie knew what was in the ammo box and why.

The Nineties—More Expansion and Acquisitions	*89*
Perfect Turn, A New Concept in Teaching Skiing	*89*
Two New Peaks	*91*
American Skiing Company and Expansion	*93*
Return of the Ski Train	*96*
Gould Sunday River, A Partnership Made Formal	*98*

The Nineties—More Expansion and Acquisitions

The 1990–91 season started with the addition of ten acres of new trails, a new race arena, and a boost in air capacity for increased snowmaking. The resort's first summit lodge opened, a 5,000-square-foot Peak Lodge and Skiing Center atop North Peak. The lodge played a key role in the introduction of the Perfect Turn Skier Development program, with 439,000 visits.

Perfect Turn, A New Concept in Teaching Skiing

In May 1988, Bob Harkins returned to Sunday River. He had started at the area as a junior patrolman during his final years at Edward Little High School in Auburn and continued as a volunteer on weekends while attending the University of Maine in Orono. On graduation from college, he became an employee at the mountain, which during those Killington years meant doing a little of everything. He worked in the rental shop, and on ski patrol, taught skiing, and coached racing. Harkins later described the routine, "It was crazy, I would be teaching a class and get an accident call."

During those years in the mid-seventies, he introduced Killington's graduated length method of teaching skiing to Sunday River and became director of racing. In 1977, he left to become athletic director, race coach, and teacher at Gould Academy. Following that job he spent the next ten years coaching racing at various levels, winding up as development coach and an assistant to Bill Marolt, U.S. Ski Team director. It was his misfortune and Sunday River's good fortune that after a disastrous 1988 Winter Olympics, he got caught up in a major restructuring of the team coaching staff.

Bob Harkins's ski career is a story by itself, but the important part is what he did with his management and ski coaching skills that he brought back to Sunday River that May in 1988. Once again performing multiple tasks from cutting trails on White Cap to grooming supervisor, Harkins was back to running the ski school when Otten presented his thoughts about ski school.

In Harkins's words, "Les looked at it from the skiers' point of view." As Otten put it, "If you make them feel good about skiing they'll come back. We run ski school on our terms. Two hour lessons are too long. It has to be accessible, convenient. Skiing is all about turning and looking good."

One of the people brought into the discussion was Rik Dow, a veteran instructor and former director of the ski school at Mount Abram. Dow introduced Harkins to Ed Joyce, an educator from Massachusetts. "We went to Ed's house in Bryant Pond and talked until 2 am," Bob recalled. That long night led to Perfect Turn.

One goal of the program was to get better skiers back into a program. The first thing Harkins and the architects of the program did was to recognize why only beginners and a handful of advanced skiers ever showed up at the ski school desk. It was the whole idea of "going back to school," they decided; no one, after all, likes to take lessons.

A Perfect Turn ski pro with rug rats.

Bob Harkins.

This is, of course, contrary to common practice in other sports: a golfer with problems goes to see the club pro, and tennis players turn to coaches. Thus the first step at Sunday River was to get rid of the dreaded "school" tag, hoping that fewer people would be put off by the label.

At the same time it was recognized that simply changing the name without restructuring would do no good. The result was the Perfect Turn. As Harkins said at the time, "We no longer have a ski school. We have a 'skier development' program." Ski instructors went the same way, becoming ski pros or coaches.

Understanding the difference calls for considering the traditional ski school. Before anyone could take a lesson, they first had to find the right level. Group lessons necessitated careful segregation of skiers by ability. Otherwise, the poorest skier in the group would suffer the embarrassment of holding up the group and the best would get bored.

The ski-off used to divide skiers was also a source of embarrassment, the pressure to ski well while being observed destroying some skiers' ability to perform. In addition, potential student skiers would picture themselves waiting around the ski school area while classes were being formed, with more waiting in the traditional group lesson. The only alternative was the expensive private lesson.

The Perfect Turn program eliminated all those factors, allowing skiers to attend clinics at their convenience. Instead of the usual 10:00 a.m. and 1:30 p.m. ski school sessions, Perfect Turn clinics would start every half hour. Skiers were classified at ten levels, the first three of which were designed to take the "never-ever" through the early stages. Those lessons started at the South Ridge Base Lodge. Levels four through ten fit skiers at various stages, beginning, intermediate, and expert. By departing every half hour from the summit (the new North Peak Lodge), the clinics made it possible to get instruction and still leave plenty of time for skiing the mountain.

According to Harkins, Perfect Turn was truly a skier development program. "One of the keys to the format," he said in that first year, "is helping skiers understand the ski as a tool." He was referring to the way experts use the ski to do the work for them. This is particularly true of racers who have contributed greatly to both technique and ski design. Whether the goal was to run gates, ski the steeps in perfect control, or just carve turns, one of the clinics could provide a starting point for developing a higher skill level.

The seventy-five-minute sessions had no more than six skiers to assure more personal attention. At the beginning of the 1990–91 season, each clinic was $15 and a special card was available for unlimited sessions.

Obviously, instructors also had to be retrained, and Rik Dow became staff development supervisor and Ed Joyce was brought on board to assist in developing proper communication. Ski pros and coaches were trained that fall in the new methods through a series of classroom and on-hill workshops before Christmas.

How well did the program work? Well enough to be franchised to other ski resorts over the years that followed.

Every year in the nineties had announcements like this.

Two New Peaks

Another peak was the big news for 1991–92. Aurora Peak opened with its own quad chair and trails. The total of sixty acres of new trails included Shock Wave, a double diamond run off White Cap, and 3-D, a new bump run off North Peak, with snowmaking on all the new terrain. The Snow Cap Inn opened with 68 guest rooms adjacent to the Snow Cap Ski Dorm, and a major expansion of the South Ridge Base Lodge included additional space for food service, ticketing, and learn-to-ski programs in a new concourse. Ski instruction continued to expand with the introduction of the Tiny Turns program for three year olds.

A celebration of the opening of the Aurora lift took place at the base of the lift in the valley behind North Peak with a gathering of skiers, press, and invited guests. For the official christening, Les Otten's administrative assistant Jolan Ippolito was designated to break the traditional bottle of champagne on the base support tower. Unfortunately, they were unaware that champagne bottles, being thicker than normal wine bottles to withstand the pressures of the sparkling wines, had to be scored before such events. The bottle failed to break on the first couple of swings. Swinging harder, Ippolito succeeded but the shattered glass cut her hand and the ski patrol got to handle its first patient on Aurora. The cut required three stitches, but the rest went smoothly under perfect blue skies and temperatures ideal for a day of skiing the new terrain. Skier visits that year exceeded a half million for the first time at 502,000.

There would be more lifts and trails to come, but the milestone of 500,000 had been crossed, and it could not have happened without the well-coordinated construction of lifts, trails, and lodging. Jolan Ippolito, who had come on board in 1982, was in the middle of the whole explosion of growth. She noted that the biggest challenge was the short window of construction and the need to hit every deadline, "It felt like we were on a merry-go-round, everything was critical, timing had to be perfect." "We had construction loans that had to be paid off. The first 36 units of Cascades Condominiums all closed in one day. It happened all the way through, with Cascades, Sunrise, South Ridge and Fall Line."

That took extraordinary coordination, between construction, sales, and financing, and it's a little-known secret of Sunday River's growth.

The big news at the start of the 1992–93 season was the opening of the new Summit Hotel and Conference Center with 147 rooms and full services. The hotel is located just east of the White Cap base, and skiers can ski down to White Cap and return to the hotel by a quad out of White Cap base. Snowmaking received the usual annual boost in capacity with increases in air and water capacity. The first move by Sunday River to expand beyond its boundaries came with the franchising of Perfect Turn to Mount Bachelor, Oregon. Skier visits totalled 525,000.

The Summit Hotel was another story of innovation. A hotel and conference center was the next logical step in order to continue on the path to a four-season resort, but the real estate market had died in 1988, making financing a challenge. Les Otten came up with the idea of quarter shares, discarding the more common selling of individual units and timeshares. Instead the buyers of the units would own thirteen weeks spread evenly through the year.

Once again the time line between coming up with the idea and making it happen was

Marketing material introducing Aurora Peak.

extremely short. In September 1991, Otten developed the concept. After a winter of selling the new concept of resort ownership, ground was broken the following May and the first Grand Summit Hotel opened for Christmas. The hotel also opened the way for true year-round operation by attracting convention business.

The biggest news of 1993 took place off the mountain with the first acquisitions of other ski resorts and the beginning operation of the Sunday River Express. In July, Sunday River purchased Attitash, a popular ski area in New Hampshire's Mount Washington Valley. A month later, Les Otten announced the intent to purchase Sugarbush in Warren, Vermont. The Perfect Turn program was franchised to two more areas, Jiminy Peak in Massachusetts and Blue Mountain in Ontario, Canada. Another move that made a big splash was the introduction of the Sunday River Silver Bullet Express, the only ski train in the east.

On the mountain, the South Ridge double was replaced by a high-speed detachable quad and a triple chair was added to bring skiers from the base of Aurora back to North Peak. Approximately sixty acres of trails and glades were added on the mountain, and a new snowboard park opened. Snowmaking received a major boost with the installation of a new high-pressure air system, giving the resort the world's largest high-pressure system. Water capacity was increased with a new reservoir. Research and development began on a new highly efficient snow gun. The south wing and ballroom opened at the Summit Hotel, upping rooms to 230. The ballroom has a capacity of 900.

At the peak of the season a fire struck, destroying the compressor building in February. This put the staff on crisis footing. With the snowmaking crippled, it would be impossible to resurface trails during the busiest month of the year. Fast action was needed. Phone calls were made to suppliers, and every company with compressors to rent was contacted. With compressors on the way, work began on the building and other equipment. Within forty-eight hours the snowmaking was up and running again. Skier visits totalled 528,000.

Recognizing that a key to a better bottom line was reducing the cost of making snow, Otten worked with Bob Ash to develop a snow gun that would produce more and better snow while using less energy. The new gun was awarded a patent, giving Sunday River a proprietary interest. This was typical of the do-it-yourself attitude at Sunday River. Not satisfied with the snowcats commercially available, Otten and his team worked in a shop in Mechanic Falls and built two frames along with tracks and sockets. Kassbohrer actually bought the idea and incorporated it into its line.

Sunday River's seventh peak was added for the 1994–95 season with a high-speed quad and a fixed-grip double serving a hundred acres of new trails in Jordan Bowl. Ninety percent of the new terrain has snowmaking, and water capacity is boosted to ensure the ability to cover the added terrain. Lodging was increased with the completion of eight new three-bedroom condo units added to the Locke Mountain Townhouses. The North Peak Lodge and Skiing Center was expanded with 1,500 square feet of additional seating.

The big marketing thrust was creation of the Edge, the first New England frequent-skier card, giving free skiing benefits at Sunday River and affiliated resorts. Those resorts got a boost when the Sugarbush purchase was completed in April 1995, and a month later the intent to buy Mount Cranmore was announced. Skier visits totalled 546,000.

Dorothy and the rest of the Oz characters on hand for the opening of Oz.

The first to ride the Aurora lift.

Evolution of the shape ski.

The off-season in 1995 began with the completion of the purchase of Mount Cranmore, making LBO Enterprises a four-resort chain. Peak number eight opened with a fixed-grip quad serving forty acres of new trails in the Oz area, with 90 percent of the new terrain served by snowmaking. Housing expansion continued with the construction of eight more three-bedroom condos in the Locke Mountain townhouse development.

Then mountain manager Chip Seamans recalled the final week of preparation for the opening of Oz. The characters from the film, including Dorothy, Tin Man, Scarecrow, and the Lion were all scheduled to be on hand when the lift opened with a bottle champagne broken over the base of the lift. The load test for the new lift was scheduled for Wednesday.

This process required of all new lifts by the state tramway board involved having four cardboard boxes representing the weight of four skiers on each chair holding plastic bags full of water. The test failed! One of the upper towers slipped, rendering the chair unusable. At that time Les Otten was more involved with the areas he was acquiring, leaving the day-to-day operations of Sunday River to his home team.

Seamans called Otten at home that night at 7:00 to pass on the bad news. He remembered the phone going silent for a time, then hearing, "How hard would we laugh if Killington [a huge rival at the time] announced they couldn't open their new gondola on schedule? Get it open."

That left Seamans sitting home alone to work out a plan. He started making phone calls to the representatives from Dopplemayer (the lift manufacturer) who were staying at the hotel. Parts would have to be flown in and all those boxes removed from a lift that was not running. They created a plan, and at 4:00 a.m., members of the ski patrol along with some of his friends from Outward Bound were climbing lift towers and sliding down the cable on ropes to knock the boxes and bags of water off the chairs. By Friday night the tower had been repaired and the load test completed. The approval from the Maine Tramway Board arrived at 9:00 a.m. Saturday, and Les Otten announced to the gathered dignitaries that another Sunday River project had been completed "on time and under budget." Skier visits totalled 589,000.

American Skiing Company and Expansion

Another year of growth at Sunday River was dwarfed by the acquisition of S-K-I Ltd. in June 1996. This purchase added Killington and Mount Snow in Vermont, Waterville Valley and Mount Cranmore in New Hampshire, and Sugarloaf in Maine under the newly formed American Skiing Company (ASC). The purchase caught the attention of the Justice Department, which ordered the divestiture of Waterville Valley and Cranmore, leaving five resorts under the ASC logo, headquartered at Sunday River.

On the mountain the high-speed quad in Jordan Bowl had its lift capacity boosted by 16 percent. Five acres of gladed terrain was added to Oz, including the double black diamond Flyin' Monkey. The annual snowmaking upgrades continued with the replacement of 150 snow guns, and research and development began on a new more efficient snow gun. Eight more three-bedroom townhouses were added in the Locke Mountain development. The guided

demo, Edge Card, and Perfect Turn programs were expanded to all ASC resorts.

The spending amounted to $1.5 million, but a press release that fall read, "We figured it was time to give our winter guests a little breather. Sunday River has grown so substantially the past five years that most skiers and riders have been unable to keep up with all the changes.

"Think about it: Since 1991, we've nearly doubled our skiable terrain with dramatic expansions onto three more mountains (Aurora Peak, Jordan Bowl, and Oz), installed six new lifts, built the Summit Hotel and Crown Club, Snow Cap Inn and more slopeside condominiums, significantly increased snowmaking coverage and expanded our base facilities—not to mention introducing several innovative new programs. In other words, enough to make one's head spin."

The following year, 1997, the high-speed detachable quad, the Perfect Turn Express, replaced the North Peak Triple, and the lift capacity of the Jordan Bowl quad was increased by 6 percent. Five new trails were added, including the double black diamond Spruce Cliffs on Spruce Peak and Northern Exposure on North Peak. Two hundred snow guns were added. The resort's expansion to the west was completed with the opening of the Jordan Grand Resort Hotel and Conference Center in December 1997 with two hundred guest rooms, two restaurants, an outdoor heated pool, spa, and day care. Other improvements were made at South Ridge, remodeling the kitchen, cafeteria, rental shop, ticketing concourse, and bathrooms. Elsewhere, Bumps! Pub, Rosetto's, and Walsh & Hill were remodeled.

While Sunday River expanded west, ASC moved west as well with the purchase of Wolf Mountain near Park City, renaming it the Canyons and agreeing to purchase Steamboat in Colorado and Heavenly straddling the California/Nevada border in South Lake Tahoe. To finance the purchase of Heavenly and Steamboat, Otten took ASC public.

The biggest news event of the 1997–98 season was delivered by the weather. A huge ice storm hit all of the Northeast, causing millions in damages from New York and into Quebec.

Skip King, who had moved from Sunday River's ski patrol director position to handling PR for the resort and finally to PR for ASC, had made a fast trip west to handle a PR challenge at Heavenly Valley. Entertainment star and California congressman Sonny Bono had died after striking a tree while skiing a glade late in the day, and King had a lot of questions to answer from the press.

On returning home on January 8, he was greeted first by a closed Route 26 after flying into Portland, with no power from Gray to Norway. At the Bethel airport he found his truck covered with five inches of ice. At the mountain, only Jordan Bowl had power, and it would be two days before South Ridge came back on line.

The biggest problem on the mountain was deicing the lifts. According to then mountain manager Bill Brown, his crews with additional help from Sugarloaf had the job of climbing the lift towers and using hammers to break the ice off the sheave wheels. He recalled listening to trees snapping with sounds like gunshots while he worked on a tower at the top of North Peak.

King related how the resort received a lot of negative PR for not only being open while thousands of Maine residents were without power, but advertising. That obscured the fact the resort had opened up the Jordan Hotel, offering shelter and hot meals to locals without power. Brown also noted that had they not operated, many of their employees would have been without paychecks along with their loss of power.

Brown pointed out how the ice storm actually increased cover and once the groomers ground up the ice, tilling into the snow beneath, good skiing returned quickly. The snowmakers took it from there, and within a week Sunday River was back to normal.

For 1998 one big change took place that skiers might not have noticed. The first chairlift, the Barker Mountain double, had been replaced by a high-speed quad in 1987, and after 11 years it was retrofitted in an almost total rebuild. That season's brochure on lifts said, "Sunday River's lift system is one of the most modern and efficient anywhere. Eighteen lifts in all . . . including four high-speed quads. One of them is brand new this year: The new Sunday River Express—faster and smoother than ever before."

The calendar that season showed how a full schedule of events had evolved over the years as the resort grew to a size that could easily host a large event with very little inconvenience to the recreational skiers on hand. It started with demo days Thanksgiving weekend and continued with FIS races, the Mel Jodrey and Meredith Wyman Langley Memorial races, the Bates Carnival, U.S. Snowboard Grand Prix Championship, NCAA championships, and the 12th Annual Bust n' Burn Mogul Competition, along with numerous other happenings and competitions.

As Sunday River's fourth decade and the century came to an end, there were no major changes to start the 1999–2000 season. Other ASC resorts needed more attention, and Sunday River had reached a level where it could be the most profitable in the chain without adding lifts or amenities.

Return of the Ski Train

The press release was headlined "The Sunday River Ski Express: passenger rail service returns to Maine!!"

That release came out on December 1, 1993, touting the initial run of train service from Portland to Sunday River, December 26. With Coors Light as a sponsor, the train was scheduled to leave Portland every day but Tuesday and Thursday at 6:45 a.m., arriving in Bethel at 8:45 a.m. with a stop in Auburn. Waiting buses would transport the four hundred skiers to the mountain and return them to the train for its 5:15 p.m. departure for the return trip.

The ski train arrives.

The train's romance was a key factor for Sunday River's president, Les Otten "There's something magical about a train. We're recapturing the excitement of the old ski trains of the 30s and 40s. Those trains made the trip as much fun as the skiing."

In addition to the fun, several pragmatic reasons were cited, including speed, convenience, and the train's weatherproof travel. Snowstorms don't stop and hardly slow down trains, a great alternative to driving in a storm. Naturally, energy efficiency and environmental friendliness were emphasized, and the train was praised by politicians and environmental groups.

Those who read the stories and showed up for that inaugural run had no idea what was involved in actually getting the train up and running. And the timeline was short indeed. It started when Carl Spangler arrived at Sunday River in August 1993.

His new boss, Les Otten, said, "I have three things I want done. Two involve skiing and the other is a train." Spangler told Otten he could handle the ski stuff but knew nothing about trains. His only connection to trains had been a rather large set he set up at Christmas, and his grandfather had been a conductor on a Pennsylvania railroad. Despite his protests, Otten simply told him to get it done because the train was going to operate that winter. And this was all while Otten was acquiring Attitash and exploring the acquisition of Sugarbush.

Spangler set about scouring the country for railroad cars, locating some in California, Pennsylvania, and a couple of other states. Otten said, "Go look at 'em." While checking out the various cars, he learned of a complete train set in Indianapolis owned by the Indiana Railway. Spangler traveled to Indiana and found seven cars from the early fifties, all totally refurbished. In the meantime, he had been searching for a company to provide service, engines, crews, and so forth, and the St. Lawrence and Atlantic, whose rails they would travel, agreed to furnish that as well.

When he showed the video he had taken to Otten and Burt Mills, they went out to see for themselves and on return told Spangler to make a deal. Indiana Railways was willing to sell all seven cars, and they bought the train set for $295,000. Then they were faced with the problem of getting seven railroad cars to Bethel from the Midwest by November 1. Canadian National was hired to move the cars to Montreal, and the St. Lawrence and Atlantic hauled them to Bethel.

Once in Bethel, the cars had to be made ready to carry skiers from Portland to Bethel. At a time of year when everyone at ski areas had a full plate getting the ski area ready to open, electricians, plumbers, mechanics, and other skilled employees were put to work on the train. Another problem was discovered immediately. Everything in the cars, including the heat, was run by electricity, and it could not be provided by the engine. A generator car had to be found. That was located in Buffalo, New York, purchased, moved to Bethel, and made ready to go.

With the train ready to go, all seemed bright. That's when the Federal Railway Administration inspectors showed up. Spangler related how they began going over the cars, checking everything from wheels and brakes to the glass windows. About the time they found the glass didn't meet safety standards and other specs weren't up to snuff, the inspectors learned the age of the cars. They came under the classification of "vintage cars," which made them exempt from many of the regulations. The crews went to work making the necessary changes, and once again things were ready to roll.

Getting the train and cars ready was only part of the equation. Skis and skiers had to be transported, not only by train but from the station in Bethel to the South Ridge Base. To transport the skiers, Sunday River purchased eight used Chicago Transit buses and cannibalized three for parts to make the other five ready for skiers. A special truck was purchased, and carts were built to haul the skis. The carts were filled with skis in Portland, loaded into a boxcar, and hauled from Bethel to Sunday River where the skiers getting off the buses found their skis waiting. With lift tickets purchased on the train, they could go directly to the slopes. It was a

The dining car.

Ambience in the lounge.

seamless operation—almost.

The target date set by Otten was Christmas, and on Christmas Day night, the train headed for Portland where everyone spent the night. At 4:00 a.m. they were at the station getting everything ready for the skiers. The inaugural run left Portland at 8 a.m. on December 26, 1993.

In four months a train was found, purchased, transported to Bethel, and prepared for service. Once again, Les Otten had taken an idea and made it work. Spangler summed it up, "That's what Les is all about, making things work."

Then we come to the "almost." The cars weren't really designed to run during Maine winters. It was difficult to get the cars warm enough, and the holding tanks for the restrooms were not adequately insulated and kept freezing up. That was a real problem, especially on the return trip when the bar car was open.

The train scored high political points with environmental groups that were Otten's opponents when he advocated widening of the Maine Turnpike. The citizens of Maine voted that expansion down in a referendum, but a decade later it was widened as the need became obvious. Route 26 from the turnpike in Gray was no bargain either, and Otten worked to get that highway upgraded with passing lanes on the hills between Gray and Oxford, work that has also since been accomplished.

One hope for the train was the opening of service from Portland to Boston on Amtrak with the idea that skiers would take that train and transfer to the Silver Bullet in Portland. That service came to be several years after the demise of the Sunday River Express. It was almost inevitable. Most adult skiers realized that the train leaving at 6:30 a.m. would arrive in Bethel at 9:00 and it would be at least 9:30 before they actually got on the mountain. They could drive the distance in an hour and a half, leave home at 6:30 and be skiing by 8:30. The result was that the only riders after the first year were kids whose parents chose to drop them off at the station rather than drive them to the mountain. The high percentage of kids with their boom boxes turned off even more adults, leaving the train filled almost entirely with kids. Of course, this also didn't do much for Coors Light as a sponsor, and revenue from the club car was far less than anticipated. The Sunday River Express lasted three seasons, was leased to Burlington Railways for summer excursions, and finally was sold to that railway. It was a great and novel idea, but skiers chose to travel by car and the kids wound up going on the weekend buses promoted by ski shops and radio stations.

Gould Sunday River, A Partnership Made Formal

Gould Academy has been a part of Sunday River from day one. Many of the founders had attended the highly rated Bethel college prep school, and faculty members, including Paul Kailey, played key roles in the building and early years of the ski area. The $10,000 in stock purchased to push the original fund drive over the top assured plenty of skiing at the area by students and faculty. The Gould ski team practiced at the area, and every afternoon students would ski from the time the classes ended until the lifts closed.

By the early nineties the need was seen for a more formal partnership between the school

The Silver Bullet Express.

and the resort. As usual, Les Otten was one of the prime movers with the idea. Along with vice president Bob Harkins, Otten met with headmaster Bill Clough to discuss a joint venture. In the spring of 1994, Clough hired Tim LaVallee, a Plymouth State skier and grad with extensive coaching experience, to rejuvenate the Gould competitive program and possibly develop a new more comprehensive program with Sunday River.

That resulted in the resort and the school deciding to combine talents and resources to create a nationally recognized academic and competitive environment. The merger of programs took place in 1995 to be known as Gould Sunday River (GSR). The goal was to give student athletes the experience of a ski academy while attending a 160-year-old college preparatory school with complete facilities and a rich tradition. Combined with the terrain and facilities at Sunday River, the students would have the best of both worlds.

An immediate goal of the program was the recruitment of talented student-athletes and building a full staff, and it didn't take long. In the fall and winter of 1996, Gould Academy constructed a state-of-the-art training and competition center at the base of Lower Cascades. The $250,000 (it would have been a lot more had P. H. Chadbourne Company of Bethel not donated native timber and pine) facility was named the Paul Kailey Competition Center, and its location was directly behind the building where he had operated the Sunri Ski Shop for so many years.

The results were impressive with an ever-growing list of skiers excelling at high levels. Freestyle skier Dominique Arsenault made the Canadian National Team during his senior year at Gould, and freestyler Marty Odlin was named to the U.S. team.

Parker Gray won two Junior Olympic overall titles and qualified for the U.S. National Alpines five times. Others who excelled were Eva Cardova, who went on to earn All-American honors in college; Carl Burnett, who made the U.S. Disabled Ski Team; and Bump Heldman, who was named to the U.S. Development Team and went on to ski for Bates College. The list is still growing, but the program wasn't only for those who would vie for U.S. team spots. In a few short years Gould achieved dominance in the New England Prep School Alpine Division I, winning the championship in 1998, 1999, 2000, 2001, 2002, and 2007.

By 2007, GSR had 16 alums working professionally within the ski industry, at numerous levels with one, Sasha Rearick, named U.S. Ski Team men's head coach.

As successful as these competitive programs were, there was more to GSR. Doug Alford, a Spanish teacher, and Rob Manning, a history teacher, direct the GSR ski patrol program. Monday afternoons students in the program spend two and a half hours training in outdoor emergency care. Tuesday through Friday they get on-the-job training working with the Sunday River Ski Patrol. Patrol director Tim Bruce praised the program, "I think it's great. What I like is the way Gould has structured the program. We try to incorporate them with our pro staff and they help us a lot. I see these kids really grow."

In addition to ski patrol and competition, a few have worked with the ski school teaching the Rug Rats, and of the normal student body of 215 students, close to two-thirds are involved in skiing at Sunday River. That's about 170 students learning a lifetime sport as an integral part of their education. For fifty years Gould has been part of Sunday River, and the GSR program (now called Gould Academy Competition Program headed by former Colby College head coach, Mark Godomsky) has made the connection even stronger.

Paul Kailey and his daughter Cindy.

A New Century, the Fifth Decade	103
The End of the Otten Eras	104
A World Record for Sunday River and Simon Dumont	106
New Era of Expansion Under Boyne	106
Snowboarding World Cup	107
New Trent Jones Jr. Course for Sunday River	109
What Is to Come?	110

A New Century, the Fifth Decade

When the new century began, Sunday River was part of the ASC family of ski areas, following the acquisitions of the nineties. The final tally included Attitash in New Hampshire; Killington, Sugarbush, and Mount Snow in Vermont; Steamboat in Colorado; the Canyons in Utah; Heavenly in California; and Maine's other giant, Sugarloaf.

The brochure that year listed:
  126 trails and glades
  18 lifts, with 4 high-speed quads
  1,300 snow guns
  12 state-of-the-art groomers
  2,340 feet of vertical descent
  155 inches of annual snowfall

2000–2001
  127 trails
 New:
  Double diamond glade
  Full-length terrain park
  500 foot competition halfpipe
  Expanded tubing park

Susan Duplessis came on as communications director in late 2000 and six weeks later found herself in the middle of one of Sunday River's biggest-ever events, the U.S. Freestyle Grand National FIS World Cup. The competition included aerials and moguls, the first on Rocking Chair and the latter on White Heat. The event attracted the best U.S. freestyle skiers, including Johnnie Moseley, Joe Pack, and Eric Bergoust and on the ladies side Carrabassett Valley Academy's Emily Cook and Brenda Petzold along with Shannon Bahrke, Ann Batelle, and Hannah Hardaway.

It was an enormous undertaking, especially for mountain operations. The mogul arena had to be created on White Heat with special grooming machines forming the bumps and jumps. The finish areas for both moguls and aerials had to be carefully laid out, giving the contestants room to come to a safe stop with corrals laid out for press and cameras. The mogul venue also had to have a judges' stand. Up on Rocking Chair the huge inruns and jumps for the aerials had to be built according to specific dimensions. The speed of the inruns has to be just fast enough to allow the aerialists to get sufficient height to perform multiple maneuvers, some inverted. But too much speed and the skiers could outjump the hill, landing on the flat and risking serious injury.

Jordan Ginsburg was the coordinator for this and many other events. At all these competitions the athletes have to be fed along with members of the press and sponsors. For this a hospitality tent was set up just below the jumps on Rocking Chair. Here various members of the press,

Sunday River's fiftieth anniversary logo.

both print and electronic, could get interviews with the athletes while refueling the body. As a member of that group, I can personally attest to the superb hospitality provided by Sunday River and the high praise the athletes, coaches, and officials had for the work of the mountain crews in preparing the venues.

In March that same year, another event took place that provided a sharp contrast for those who had attended a similar event in 1982. The Eastern Ski Writers returned for their annual meeting, and the group included a number who had attended the meeting twenty years before. As related earlier, that first meeting in early December had skiing only on the Mixing Bowl and the writers stayed at the Bethel Inn some six miles from the mountain.

This time lodging was at the brand-new Jordan Grand Resort Hotel with its ski-in/ski-out convenience. Instead of a single run, all 127 runs and glades were open with packed powder everywhere. Duplessis recalled, "The ESWA event was a ton of planning and we couldn't have asked for better weather. When I first met the group I realized that so many of the writers had not been to Sunday River in years, and had not even seen the expansion out to Aurora, Oz, and Jordan. I wanted so desperately to impress the group and as usual, had the backing of the mountain ops crew in making sure the snow was in the best possible condition. Mother Nature shined on us, too, and we had beautiful conditions and weather. I think the writers were truly, truly impressed with the expansion of the resort and the commitment to guest service and the snow."

What a difference twenty years and millions of dollars can make.

Another night life option at Sunday River.

The End of the Otten Eras

When ASC expanded west with the purchase of Steamboat and Heavenly, the idea was to provide insurance against the weather. A bad snow year in the east could be offset by business in the west. It made sense, but the first two years were poor snow years both east and west. The resulting losses led to borrowing, and Les Otten lost control of the company, finally leaving in March 2001. A year later ASC, now fully controlled by Oak Hill, moved its headquarters to Park City in Utah and eventually decided to get out of the ski business entirely by selling off the resorts.

The brochure announcing the beginning of the 2006–07 season was the last to list Sunday River as part of the American Skiing Company resorts. The trail count had risen to 131, but little else had changed since the turn of the century.

When it came time for ASC to sell Sunday River, the package also included Sugarloaf. The purchaser was CNL Income Properties Inc., a real estate investment trust. The resorts were leased to Boyne Resorts, a Michigan company with over sixty years in the ski business operating resorts in Utah, Washington, British Columbia, and Montana along with Boyne and Boyne Highlands in its home state.

About the time of closing, a once-in-a-lifetime rain (seven to eight inches in forty-five minutes) hit Newry and gave Sunday River a massive job just repairing the damage in time for the season opening. As Joe Aloisio, the company engineer who would oversee much of the

Les Otten.

repairs, told the story, "The big rain storm started late at night on July 11th and continued into the early morning of July 12th. We had major damage to the road and sewer as you drive up to the North Peak Condominiums. The hole along the side of the road was up to 25 feet deep. The culverts at the South Ridge and White Cap base areas were damaged and required replacement. When the White Cap culvert was damaged the water ran across the base area undermining the front towers of lift 11 (the lift from White Cap base to the hotel). To repair the lift it was necessary to remove tension from the cable and remove the lift towers before we could put everything back together. The culvert at Brookside Condominiums was completely destroyed and required replacement along with rebuilding the trail. Then there was the Barker base area. Many of the culverts above the base were destroyed, sending more rocks, soil and water into the pond at Barker. The culvert there could not handle the volume and ripped itself apart. When it did this it took most of the earth between the base lodge and the pump house with it, leaving a crater that stretched from building to building that was 20 feet deep. To repair that area we had to jack up the base lodge, and relocate the numerous snowmaking pipes that run from the pump house in that area."

The Grand Summit Hotel.

The rain came so fast that the runoff overwhelmed everything in its path. It took out the culvert under the road between the lower part of the Barker parking lot and the Sunrise Condominiums, continued down the brook behind Viking Village and took out a large section of road near the entrance to the Brookside Condominiums, and did its final damage to the road into the Grand Summit Hotel. The water coming from South Ridge did major damage to the road into the Cascades Condominiums just below the base lodge.

Bill Brown told me on May 21, 2009, nearly two years after the event, that two days before he had retrieved a snow gun and two sets of hoses that had been buried by the runoff on Top Gun. No one knows how much more was buried by the rocks and mud when the deluge hit the mountain, but everyone knows the work was completed in time to open in November.

The $2.5 million required for the cleanup and repair was plenty to do before opening, but the first of October the resort announced another $4.8 million in upgrades, with $1 million going into snowmaking. Other improvements were made to the two hotels, condos, and the Snow Cap Inn and Ski Dorm.

The 2007–2008 brochure no longer mentioned ASC. Instead a box on the inside of the back cover reads as follows:

"Introducing Boyne Rewards, a program rewarding skiers for every dollar spent at any Boyne resort with points good at all of the resorts, Big Sky in Montana, Boyne Mountain and Boyne Highlands in Michigan, Brighton in Utah, Crystal Mountain in Washington, Cypress Mountain in Vancouver and Sugarloaf in Maine."

Chapter Six: 2000s

A World Record for Sunday River and Simon Dumont

The biggest event of 2007–2008 happened near the end of the season. Bethel native Simon Dumont returned to the area where he had honed his skills to make an attempt on the world record for height off a quarter pipe. The feature was built on Airglow, a black diamond run off Aurora on a flat area at the bottom of a headwall. On April 11, Dumont roared down at 55 miles per hour and launched into the air off the 38-foot feature. His jump of 35.5 feet above the rim was officially recognized by the Guiness Book of World Records.

Sunday River's Nick Lambert explained the event and the logistics, "It was great that Simon wanted to attempt the record at Sunday River after skiing in the biggest contests and on the biggest jumps all over the world. On the resort side it took the coordination of a lot of people, equipment and snow to pull it off. When he broke the record there were 50 people on site including three photographers and four film crews, a two-ton crane with an 85-foot camera boom, a rope tow set up specifically for the event, a 50-foot height meter on top of the quarter pipe, and more Red Bull than we could possibly drink in a year."

The jump wasn't a simple leap into the air. Dumont threw a "corked 900 (2.5 spins) with a tail grab to make an incredible picture high over the rim of the pipe."

It was only natural that Dumont would return to Sunday River to make his record try. He had started skiing there at the age of three and began to get recognition for this free skiing skills at the age of ten. Further honing his skills through his high school years, Dumont made his debut at the age of fourteen in the 2000 Winter X Games.

At seventeen, in 2003, he devoted himself to full-time competition, winning the Whistler Invitational Super Hit. The following year he soared to the top of the pack taking gold in the Winter X Games Superpipe and placing first at the Ultimate Bumps and Jumps Quarterpipe, among many other awards. From that time on, the Sunday River "Newschool" skier dominated the competition, winning around the world. When not in competition, Dumont appeared in movies and videos, becoming the most recognized skier ever to come out of Bethel and Sunday River.

Bethel's own Simon Dumont sets the world record for height.

New Era of Expansion Under Boyne

One year later, under Boyne, Sunday River announced an expansion that was big even when compared with some of the big growth years of the eighties and nineties. Included in the $14

New England's first Chondola, combining eight-passenger gondala cabins and six-passenger chairs.

million plan was $7.2 million for a "Chondola," the first of its kind in New England. The new lift would replace the triple out of South Ridge, but rather than drop skiers just above the base of the Spruce Peak triple, it extended to a point above the North Peak Lodge. The hybrid lift combined six passenger chairs with eight passenger gondola cabins, with four chairs between each cabin.

For the first time the grand opening of a new lift at Sunday River was held at night under newly installed lights, demonstrating the multiple uses of the lift. "This is the day we have all been waiting for," said Dana Bullen, general manager. "The Chondola changes the way we interact with our guests. It accommodates both skiers and snowboarders and can handle much more volume."

The versatility of the new lift was further demonstrated as nonskiers and nonboarders loaded for the initial ride to the top, 5,994 feet away, where the first gourmet dinner would be served. While speeding access to the mountain out of South Ridge was an important benefit, the new lift was expected to play a key role in giving guests an opportunity to enjoy a mountaintop dinner. In addition, as a means of transport for guests on foot the Chondola was a major step in expanding Sunday River's summer business. Boyne brought years of experience operating year-round resorts to its new resort in the western Maine mountains, and Stephen Kircher, president of eastern operation for the company made it clear that more year-round activity was in Sunday River's future.

Snowboarding World Cup

Sunday River's first Snowboarding World Cup event.

Sunday River wrapped up February with a giant snowboard event, a Snowboard World Cup. A parallel giant slalom on Monday Mourning on the first day provided plenty of excitement, which could be seen from the second-floor deck of Barker Base Lodge. The runs were also visible on the huge Jumbotron for those watching near the finish area. Fog delayed the race everyone was waiting for, the Snowboard Cross with Farmington Olympic gold medalist Seth Wescott the favorite. Unfortunately, Wescott got a poor start in the final and failed to make up the time. But the crowd saw plenty of action on the course that started on Lower Punch and finished right in front of the base lodge on lower Rocking Chair.

The course was designed by Jeff Ihaksi, who laid out the course at the Torino Olympics and was chosen to design the course for the 2010 winter games in Vancouver. To build the banked turns and rolling jumps took tons of man-made snow, hundreds of man-hours, and many hours of grooming machines shaping the features.

Vice president of marketing Jim Costello felt that the six-figure investment would pay off in TV exposure. Most of the skiers and snowboarders watching with lift tickets would have bought them anyway, and for those on foot there was no charge, and it's unlikely they spent enough in the base lodge to make a dent in the expense of hosting the event. As a showcase for the U.S. Ski and Snowboard Team it was definitely a success, and at the same time it highlighted the capabilities of the Sunday River team in hosting such a high-profile event.

The month of March featured a return of the NCAA championships with the giant slalom

and slalom at Sunday River and the cross-country at Black Mountain in Rumford. The 24th Annual Ski-A-Thon took place on March 21 and raised close to $300,000, keeping that program well funded.

New Trent Jones Jr. Course for Sunday River

Spectacular views from every hole.

The big news in 2004 was aimed at summer. Five years earlier Les Otten and Joe Aloisio had pored over topographical maps and walked the land off the access road to Jordan Bowl, locally an extension of the Monkey Brook Road. They had outlined a 350-acre site and located tee and green locations. Then Robert Trent Jones Jr. was brought in to design and plan a golf course on the site.

The design was created to complete the year-round package of the resort along with the building of the Jordan Grand Resort Hotel and Conference Center. Logging off the fairways actually got underway at that time, but the project had been on hold while the parent ASC worked on other priorities. Through a partnership with Harris Golf Company construction moved forward. Led by well-known Maine pro Dick Harris and his two sons, Jeff and Jason, Harris Golf operated Bath and Boothbay Country Clubs and Maine's largest golf shop in South Portland. They would build, own, and operate the new course.

Located just off the access road to the hotel, the 350-acre site occupies a northwest-facing hillside allowing the designer to create a variety of holes, at least half with views of the sharp Mahoosuc Range ridgeline across the valley. Jones described the site, "The Jordan Bowl area at Sunday River provides one of the most unique landscapes for a golf course in New England. The combination of mountain terrain and native forested vegetation will set the stage for one of the most outstanding courses we have had the opportunity to develop."

With ample acreage the designer was able to lay out eighteen separate self-contained fairways. The track follows the natural topography to maximize views and terrain features with dramatic elevation changes.

The Mahoosuc Range as a backdrop.

When he designed Sugarloaf in the early eighties the world-famous architect said that layout would be the most challenging in New England, the only exception at the time being the Country Club in Brookline when it was set up for the U.S. Open. In the two decades since, a lot of courses have been built in New England but Sugarloaf still holds its own in challenge. When asked about the inevitable comparisons, Jones noted that the Sunday River course would have wider fairways than its sister resort, making it more friendly. He added "We're going to strike a balance between challenge and playability. We'll put the fairway bunkers out where only the big boys can reach them."

With sixty-plus bunkers everyone has an opportunity to use their sand irons, but four sets of tees allow the shorter hitters to come in with more lofted clubs to reduce the margin of error. The big hitters need length and accuracy from the tips at 7,130 yards, while the rest can choose between 6,558, 5,828, and 5,006. A check of the par seventy-two scorecard shows the par fives playing 520–575 from the back tees and par threes ranging from 205 down to 150 from the front.

Due to the sloping location and the well-drained soil there is little water on the course. Merrill Brook divides the front and back nines but doesn't come into play. Traps, doglegs, and elevation changes make up for the lack of water along with carries over other hazards to reach landing areas from the back sets of tees on some holes. Other holes have the distance to make them intimidating. Seventeen and eighteen playing 475 from the back are the kinds of par fours that create a demanding finish.

The "wilderness lodge" clubhouse fits the surroundings with natural stone and wood inside and out. The Robert Trent Jones II Grille serves everything needed for après golf along with lunch and dinner, and the well-stocked pro shop offers the top brands. The deck that runs the entire length of the clubhouse overlooks the putting green, the first tee, and ninth green, all with the spectacular backdrop of the Mahoosuc Range, an ideal setting to enjoy that post-round libation. A complete range and practice area headquarters the golf school.

Since its opening, Sunday River Golf Club has been recognized as being a top public play course, by *Golf Digest* ("Top Ten New Public Courses in the Country"), *Travel & Leisure Golf* ("Top Ten New Courses Worldwide"), *Golf Magazine*, and *Golf Styles New England*, among others.

What Is to Come?

As the first fifty years came to a close, Sunday River attracted 586,000 skier visits in the 2008–2009 season. The company that had started on leased land on Barker Mountain was now a resort with 10,000 acres of private land spread over a range of peaks. Dana Bullen had been general manager since 2003, and Jim Costello was vice president of sales and marketing after coming over from Sugarloaf in 2002. Stephen Kircher, president of eastern operations for Boyne, was overseeing operations at Loon, Sugarloaf, and Sunday River.

Dana Bullen summed up his tenure at the resort, "Les's shoes were completely unfilled, and they were monstrous shoes." This echoed the thoughts of Kircher and Costello, along with many others. Everyone agreed that the lift system, snowmaking, grooming, lodging, and infrastructure was exceptional, able to handle 600,000 skiers annually without stretching.

Reflecting on the assets of Sunday River, Kircher noted "the vastness of the property and long term potential, great variety of terrain, good location and the Bethel community." On expansion he cited the untapped capacity within the current footprint and beyond. The resort could handle another 100,000 skier visits without expanding the current boundaries.

A lone mountain biker challenges the mountain in the summer.

Kircher described the snowmaking plant as extraordinarily powerful, especially air. It was state of the art twenty years ago and easily adaptable to efficiency. He also admired the staff as having a lot of talented people who believed in the place and were dedicated and committed to its future. Boyne would not be making wholesale changes. In fact, the parent company was taking some things from Sunday River. In places Boyne would take away from the Maine resort, and in others inject its methods and technology. The vision was a combining of the best of both resorts.

A major goal for the next decade was the creation of a viable four-season resort. With a new lift and increased snowmaking in place, Bullen and his team were working on amenities such as improved food offerings and better connectivity of trails for mountain biking. With the Androscoggin River cleaned up and the Sunday River along with other streams in the area available, fly-fishing was added to the summer mix and the resort was working with inland fisheries and game to best use the part of the 10,000 acres outside the ski area boundaries.

As to how the resort fits into the region, Bullen responded, "Boyne understands that Sunday River is part of the Bethel area. We want to complement the area not compete with it." One challenge is how to get skiers into the village of Bethel. Most skiers arrive from Route 26 and take the parkway shortcut that bypasses the town entirely. Only by detouring through the town or returning after ski hours do skiers see the old homes, the Bethel Inn on the common, and the campus of Gould Academy, a school that played a key role in Sunday River from the very beginning.

Looking into the future we can expect to see more cooperation between the local area and the resort. Whether it comes from having local restaurants open on the mountain or working with local recreational opportunities, the vision is one of sharing Sunday River guests with the Bethel area.

The Jordan Grand Hotel in summer.

Kircher had a few specifics but suggested growth would be incremental rather than explosive, that a comprehensive master plan would involve all aspects of the resort. Some ideas being discussed included a multicourse golf operation, creating an energy hub at South Ridge, replacing White Cap base with lodging, an array of outdoor adventure, and conferences centered on nature. The pace of change would be determined by the availability of capital as the end of the first half century came during an economic downturn. But from those humble beginnings fifty years previously, Sunday River has grown into one of the busiest ski resorts in New England, and the potential for further growth is apparent.

Trail Map

Sunday River at a Glance

1,900+ SNOW GUNS
92 PERCENT TERRAIN COVERAGE
167+ INCHES AVERAGE ANNUAL SNOWFALL

8 Peaks / 132 Trails and Glades

44 GREEN CIRCLE
47 BLUE SQUARE
25 BLACK DIAMOND
16 DOUBLE BLACK DIAMOND

4 TERRAIN PARKS
1 SUPERPIPE
1 MINI-PIPE
16 LIFTS
1 CHONDOLA

4 HIGH-SPEED QUADS
5 FIXED QUADS
3 TRIPLES
1 DOUBLE
2 SURFACE